Stefan Einhorn is professor and chair of the Ethics Council at the Karolinska Institute in Stockholm. He has written books in the fields of popular medicine and the philosophy of religion.

THE ART OF BEING KIND

STEFAN EINHORN

Translated by NEIL SMITH

sphere

SPHERE

First published in Great Britain in 2006 by Sphere
This paperback edition published in 2008 by Sphere

A CIP catalogue record for this book
is available from the British Library.

ISBN 978-0-7515-4018-5

Papers used by Sphere are natural, recyclable products made from
wood grown in sustainable forests and certified in accordance
with the rules of the Forest Stewardship Council

Typeset in Bembo by M Rules
Printed and bound in Great Britain by
Clays Ltd, St Ives plc
Paper supplied by Hellefoss AS, Norway

Sphere
An imprint of
Little, Brown Book Group
100 Victoria Embankment
London EC4Y 0DY

An Hachette Livre UK Company

www.littlebrown.co.uk

*For my family, my friends and
my colleagues – for all that you have done
and all that you do*

It is one of the beautiful compensations of life that no man can sincerely try to help another without helping himself.

Ralph Waldo Emerson

CONTENTS

INTRODUCTION

When I arrived at the clinic that morning I realised straight away that the atmosphere was tense. 'What's happened?' I asked the receptionist. She gave me a worried look before replying: 'One of your patients died during the night. The doctor on call was here a little while ago and was telling anyone who'd listen that he had encouraged the relatives to report you to the disciplinary board. Otherwise he would do it himself. The relatives are evidently furious with you.'

I understood at once which patient it was. The day before I had been visited at the clinic by a sprightly lady of about seventy-five, with inquisitive eyes. She had her son with her. We had not met before, and she was there to receive a second chemotherapy treatment for her cancer. She had a form of lymphoma, sometimes known as cancer of the lymphatic system, which, untreated, would be fatal, but with treatment we can cure about half of all patients. After the first treatment she had had heart problems and had been admitted for observation, but now she felt fine and was ready for her next treatment. We had a long conversation, during which I explained, amongst other things, the risks to her heart of a new treatment, but also that this was her only chance of being cured. She replied that she was aware of the risks, and that she wanted to continue the treatment. When I suggested that she stay overnight on the ward after the treatment, she declined, saying that she wanted to leave when it was over. She was going to stay with her son, and thought that was observation enough. I did not insist.

As we stood in the doorway at the end of the consultation, she looked at me with a smile and said: 'Well, you're a very nice doctor, for taking the time to speak to an old lady when your waiting room is full of patients.'

'It's really not a problem – it was nice to meet you,' I replied, thinking that if I worked through my lunch-hour I would just about have caught up in time for the afternoon clinic.

She had been brought in during the night with heart problems, and the duty doctor had admitted her to a ward. A few hours later she had been found dead in her bed.

That a patient should die is not unusual when you work with cancer. It always makes me sad, but this was something different. That a patient should die as a result of a mistake on my part felt extremely difficult. I went through what had happened. To administer the treatment was, in my opinion, the correct decision, because the patient herself had been positive about it, despite being aware of the risks. But I could have insisted on admitting her. Why had I not done so?

With these thoughts whirling round in my head, I went off to phone the woman's son. As he picked up the phone and I said who I was, I braced myself for an outburst of recriminations, and was therefore extremely taken aback when he said: 'I'm glad you called. I wanted to thank you for the way you looked after my mother.' He told me what had happened during the night, and how he and the other relatives were feeling. We spoke for a while about what had happened, and about his mother.

Then I told him that I was being criticised for the way in which I had treated his mother, and that I myself now felt that I should have insisted on her being admitted. To my surprise he replied: 'But you did. You insisted on her being admitted, but Mum refused. That's my recollection, and if you're reported then I shall say so on record.' Surprised by his support, and at the fact that my recollection was so wrong, I emphasised at the end that they were welcome to call if there was anything they wanted to ask about in the future. He was silent for a moment, then said: 'There's something you should know, Stefan. Mum said she didn't like that duty doctor, but that you had been so kind to her. That's why I shan't do anything that might harm you.' After the conversation ended, I sat for a while by the telephone thinking about what he had said. There was nothing wrong with my memory of the conversation with his mother. The son knew that I had not insisted on admission. He had chosen to protect me.

I was never reported – the opinion of the senior physician was that I had not committed any formal errors, while the duty doctor in turn ought to have asked a cardiologist to examine the patient. But if the relatives had reported me, I would have been forced to go through the whole process of reports back and forth to the National Board of Health and Welfare, and many months of uncertainty. I had saved myself from all of this because I had been perceived as being kind.

I have had reason to consider the concept of 'kindness' many times. As a child I was often told, like so many others: 'That wasn't very kind' or 'You must be kind to your sister'. Where adults are concerned, however, the word kind appears in different contexts. 'Yes, he's kind, but so are cows in the field' is one Swedish expression, or: 'The only good thing you can say about her is that she's kind.' Or what about this one: 'Well, I suppose she's quite kind.'

So what about the concept of being 'kind'? Is it a positive or a negative attribute? Is it good or bad to be kind? With adults, it often seems as though the concept of being 'kind' is linked to behaviour which is regarded as infantile or immature. A kind person is seen as a bit 'backward', or weak, someone who does not dare raise objections. A kind adult is assumed to be a wimp. Children, on the other hand, are permitted to be kind.

And what about the word 'good', which to me is almost synonymous with being kind? 'A good person' is a phrase we almost never hear, except perhaps about the deceased. When someone is described as good, it is often in an ironic tone.

How has this happened? How have words such as 'kind' and 'good' become negatively loaded? Every time I hear that disparaging tone it surprises me, and I wonder whether the speaker has realised who has best understood what is important in life. It is time for a paradigm shift in the way we view kind people.

For me, a kind person is someone who lives with ethics in their heart. A kind person carries within their consciousness a constant concern for their fellow human beings. To my mind, this seems like an extremely good characteristic. And a kind person is least of all stupid. On the contrary, a kind person is very wise, because they – consciously or unconsciously – have realised what it is all about: that what we do to our fellows, we also do to ourselves.

We have everything to gain from being good towards those around us, and a lot to lose by not being good. A person who is kind is on the path to success. In fact I believe kindness to be the single most important factor when it comes to how successful we will be in our lives. So if we are not kind for any other reason, we should be kind for our own sake – so that we can be successful in our lives. Or, as the American author James Freeman Clarke more formally expressed it: 'See to do good, and you will find that happiness will run after you.'

The interesting thing is that this applies not just to individuals, but also to groups, organisations and societies. If we study different episodes in human history, it can sometimes seem that this is not the case. Ruthless and totalitarian states have sometimes been able to oppress more ethical societies. But these gains generally prove themselves to be short-lived, and pretty often lead to the demise of the bad societies. It is my view that the good, nurturing groups win in the long run.

Being kind is not always simple to put into practice. Always letting others have their way, for instance, is not the same as being kind, especially when others are wrong and the consequences of their actions could be negative. Nor is kindness the same as being spineless and letting yourself be exploited by others. Or volunteering to do things that are against your nature.

Kindness is a quality that must be handled with a great deal of discernment. And in exceptional circumstances you might have to do things that others may in the short term perceive as being less than good. This is part of the reason why I have chosen to write about the *art* of being kind. Being kind in a genuine, positive and good way is truly an art.

There are those who claim that humankind is fundamentally evil. And that much that takes place between people is evil. I do not agree. My perception is quite the opposite:

most of what we do for one another is good. The great majority of people strive to do what is fundamentally the right thing.

I lecture a great deal on ethics and about how we should treat our fellow human beings. As an introduction, I usually ask the audience a question – what quality would they most want to have? I usually let them choose between being intelligent, creative, highly qualified for their work, funny, and occasionally I also add wealthy (even if this is not a quality). They can also choose the quality of being a good person. More than 90 per cent of the audience usually choose this last option. This figure speaks for itself: we prioritise being good, even above endless wealth or super-intelligence.

And because there are already a large number of books that deal with how to become rich, smart, creative, qualified for your work, and so on, I thought there ought to be at least one book about how to develop the art of being kind, and about how we can be successful through being good.

People speak about normal intelligence and emotional intelligence. The former refers to our capacity for analytical thought, and the latter to our ability to handle a situation emotionally. I believe there is also another form of intelligence – ethical intelligence. Our ethical IQ indicates our capacity for doing good. This capacity is partly inherited and partly developed during our earliest years. But this is a form of intelligence that we can go on to develop throughout adulthood. And this is an important form of intelligence, because it is a basic factor in how successful we will be in our lives.

In the opening chapters I shall discuss the concepts of kindness, ethics and goodness. I shall also discuss common pitfalls we must avoid if we want to be truly kind. Then I shall present the argument that we have a lot to gain by being kind. In a later chapter I shall discuss what success is and how we can define this diffuse concept. After that I shall be so presumptuous as to give actual advice on how we can use our goodness, our ethics, our kindness, in order to be successful in our lives.

The book can be read from cover to cover, but it is also fine to take a less structured approach and read extracts from it here and there. After all, people are interested in different things, and in different ways.

I must stress one important factor – however obvious it may seem. It would be natural to ask if I am a living example of how a kind person ought to be. The answer is no, but that I am constantly trying to learn more about how to live a kind life.

There are no perfect people, and we should be on our guard against those who believe themselves to be faultless. The day we think we are our own ideal is the day we must start again from scratch. Being a thoroughly good person is a mirage – we may well strive for it, but, like seeking the pot of gold at the end of the rainbow, we will never reach it. But we can decide to become better people, in the knowledge that we will never be perfect. And, in the end, all we can do is our best.

ON KINDNESS AND ETHICS

One day a good friend phones you in tears. She is happy with her husband, but he is very jealous. She has just had dinner with her previous partner. The meeting was entirely innocent, but her husband has found out that they have been seen in town and is furious. Your friend begs you to say that the two of you had been out together that evening and that her former partner turned up quite by chance for a short while. Can you imagine lying for your old friend's sake?

A colleague hasn't performed her work as well as usual over recent months. When you speak to her about it she reveals that her son is suffering from severe mental illness and has tried to commit suicide. She makes you promise not to tell anyone. Some weeks later you meet your boss, who says he is planning to fire your colleague, and that the board will make a decision that afternoon.

Your protests do no good, but you believe his heart would soften if you told the truth. You cannot get hold of your colleague. Do you break the promise and tell your boss?

In our society we have norms and principles that we ought to follow. Not telling lies is a norm on which we can all agree. But on the other hand we ought to – according to another norm – stick up for our friends. It might look like an expression of kindness to lie for a good friend's sake, but is it acceptable to tell a lie?

In much the same way, it is a norm in our society to keep promises. A promise must not be broken. But, on the other hand, we occasionally end up in situations where greater goodness can be fostered if we break this norm.

We can argue back and forth from both sides of these dilemmas. Whatever we do, it will be both right and wrong. There is an area of philosophy which deals with how we should analyse and act when faced with different dilemmas – ethics. Ethics has its roots many thousands of years back in time. As I see it, the areas of kindness and ethics overlap in many different ways.

For this reason I believe it is important for us to spend a short while thinking about what kindness and ethics mean, about what the preconditions are for acting in a good way, and about how we can develop this capacity.

Ethics

The term 'ethics' can be defined in various ways. As I see it, ethics is always about relationships – with our fellow human beings, with the animals we share this biosphere with, and actually with the whole of the planet. Ethics is about taking responsibility for these relationships. So I define ethics as *the way in which we relate to our fellow human beings and our surroundings*. This definition also underlines the fact that the adoption of ethical positions is not unusual in our everyday life. Ethics is not only about matters of life and death. Every time we encounter another human being, we also encounter ethics. How shall I relate to this individual? How can I best meet their needs? How much time can I spare? What consequences will my actions have? Should I see my fellow human being as an object or as an individual? Ethics therefore deals with the art of being a (fellow) human being.

According to my definition, however, our responsibility stretches much further than this. We also have a responsibility for the whole of the planet, with its myriad life-forms – both animal and vegetable. We hold in our hands the potential to make the world blossom, and the capacity to lay waste to it. Ethics is therefore a fundamental basis for our capacity for doing good, for a humanistic society, for our ability to survive as a species, and for the survival of the entire planet.

'Moral' is a term often used when it comes to questions of good or evil. Originally there was no major difference between the concepts of morals and ethics, because both words mean *custom* or *practice* in Greek and Latin respectively. But over time these terms have come to mean slightly different things. One definition of ethics is: 'The external norms, laws and rules that we are expected to follow.' Ethics, according to this definition, is the framework within which we move as individuals. Morals, in turn, can be defined as: 'The practical way of dealing with ethical choice situations', which means that morals deal with how we think and act as individuals in the face of an ethical problem.

Now that we have defined these terms, we can move on to state that it is common – and that it functions fairly well – to use the words pretty much as we like, and to talk, for instance, of 'inner ethics' or 'societal morals'. The important thing to remember is that each term refers to relationships.

John, a pensioner, collapses in the street. Immediately a group of people gathers round him, an ambulance is called, and he is offered some fruit juice, because he explains that he is diabetic and has forgotten to take his medication.

Little Joe is standing crying his heart out in a large shopping centre, and soon several people come up to him and make sure he has company, and that his mother is informed over the loudspeaker.

Elaine's husband unexpectedly dies of a heart attack, and she suddenly discovers how many friends she has, who make sure that she does not have to be alone in her grief.

When Anna passes a group of noisy teenagers on the underground she notices that one of them is following her. She is very frightened by the time he catches up with her and hands her the purse that had fallen out of her handbag.

There are plenty of examples of people showing goodness and consideration to one another. But why is it that we are good towards our fellows in the vast majority of situations? Why do we not simply murder our neighbour when he starts up his lawnmower at seven o'clock on a Saturday morning? Why do we not steal an unlocked car on the street if it is nicer than ours? Why are we generally fair, friendly and considerate towards our fellow human beings?

The answer is that we don't really know. Religious leaders may claim that the reason is that there is a divine 'natural law' which means that good deeds get their reward while bad deeds are punished, and that the ability to distinguish good from evil has been instilled in us.

Evolutionary biologists, in turn, may claim that mankind is gifted with the capacity for ethical/moral thought because it lends an advantage in the struggle for survival. We would have exterminated ourselves at an early stage, or fallen prey to other animals, if we had not been able to cooperate and defend ourselves.

The sociologists may claim that it is a matter of social convention, which means that we have agreed to treat one another well because everyone gains by this. These norms, rules and laws are then passed from generation to generation as a result of each new crop of children being taught them by their parents and the society to which they belong.

It might, of course, be the case that everyone is right, and that the capacity to be good has reached us in several different ways. It could be like a car with two brake systems: if we don't get the capacity one way, there'll be a back-up system.

Ethical dilemmas are common

An ethical dilemma is a situation in which the alternative courses of action available to us have both advantages and disadvantages. However we act, it is likely to be both right and wrong at the same time.

In many countries, including the UK, there is an ongoing debate about the extent to which euthanasia ought to be allowed. Euthanasia means ending a severely ill person's life, for example by administering a fatal dose of a drug. In Sweden, opinion polls have shown that the general population is better disposed towards active euthanasia than doctors and nurses tend to be. Without going into this debate in detail, we can see that this is an example of an ethical dilemma where there are both advantages and disadvantages in either allowing or forbidding active euthanasia. According to legislators in Sweden and the UK, the disadvantages outweigh the advantages, and therefore active euthanasia remains forbidden.

But ethics is not only about euthanasia, or about whether it is right to kill someone in order to save the lives of others, or about whether the global community should act on suspicions of genocide. Ethical dilemmas are considerably more common than that.

A few years ago a friend of mine was working for a small company. In total there were six employees, besides the boss, who was the founder of the company. The sales director had been working with the boss for almost twenty years. They knew each other very well, and their families often spent time together.

The sales director was by this time over sixty, and having increasing difficulty keeping up with developments, particularly in the area of IT. His mistakes became more common and he sometimes seemed confused. The boss was naturally concerned about the situation, and his colleagues suggested with increasing frequency that something had to be done. The boss did not have the heart to dismiss his old friend and colleague so close to his retirement, and eventually chose to employ an assistant, who in reality took over responsibility for many of the sales director's tasks. At the same time the business climate worsened and the company's turnover began to fall. The cost of the extra employee, which meant that two people were in effect doing one man's job, contributed to the fact that the business went bankrupt. All the employees lost their jobs.

Is this a good example of a wrong decision taken in the

face of an ethical dilemma? Perhaps the company could have been saved if the boss had been tougher and had simply dismissed his old friend. Then six people would have kept their jobs, instead of seven losing them and the company going bust. From this simple piece of mathematics, the answer seems obvious.

But ethics is not always a question of simple maths. It is easy to be wise after the event. The boss could not possibly have known that the company would go bankrupt. He assumed they could afford to employ one extra person. This was not the case, and how realistic this hope was it is difficult to know. If it had succeeded, we would probably be praising the manager for his warm-hearted attitude towards his friend and colleague.

On the other hand, we might think that the dismissal of the sales director could have had positive consequences for him. Maybe he hated his job, but felt he had to continue so as not to let down his boss and the company which seemed to need him. Perhaps he had a suspicion that he was no longer really suited to his job. In time it might have been a relief for him to have left the company. With hindsight, we can perhaps say that the best thing in this situation would have been to dismiss him in order to save the other jobs.

Or would it? Perhaps the business would have failed anyway. Then his dismissal would have been merely an unnecessary gesture, with all the emotional consequences this would have had for the faithful old employee.

Ultimately the answer is that there was no definite answer

at the time the decision was taken. This is typical for an ethical dilemma. Sometimes it is a matter of making probability calculations – what will the probable consequences be if I act this way or that? Sometimes it is a matter of following norms and rules, and sometimes of breaking these principles. Sometimes it means weighing negative consequences for some people against positive effects for others. It can also be about how much you should look after yourself and your own interests in relation to other people's.

This is an example of an ethical dilemma where the decision had widespread consequences. But ethical dilemmas can be about situations where the consequences are not as dramatic.

Over the past few summers, my children have spent a few weeks at summer camp. One summer I went over there for the day, to see what it was like. My children had begged me to bring some crisps, sweets and fizzy drinks with me. When I arrived I was met by the man who ran the place. He looked at my bag and said: 'You know it's not allowed to bring sweets for the kids? It's a question of fairness.' I replied that I understood. When I met my kids a bit later and explained that I couldn't give them any of the things I had brought, they looked at me with sad, disappointed eyes. I went back to the car and – with a guilty conscience – put away what I had brought. A couple of hours passed, and I felt in my heart that I had acted wrongly, although I had followed norms and rules that I felt were reasonable. But they were my children, and there was a sad look in their eyes. Eventually I went and got the fizzy drinks and the crisps (he had only mentioned 'sweets') and discreetly gave them to my children. I knew that I had acted incorrectly according to the rules, but it was with a lighter heart that I hugged my kids and drove away.

Rules, norms and principles exist to be followed, but sometimes we find ourselves in situations where other ethical aspects have to be taken into account. I knew I was doing wrong by breaking the rules, but, in the situation I was in, I nevertheless chose to do so. In that situation there was no obvious solution. I chose one alternative that was both right and wrong, and discarded another which was both right and wrong.

Ethical dilemmas are commonplace. It might be a question of stopping to help someone whose car has broken down and thereby risking getting home late. Or taking the time to wash your mug in the staffroom and being late for a meeting. Or making the effort to say hello to a colleague down the corridor instead of sneaking into your room when you arrive tired first thing in the morning.

We can see that ethics form part of our everyday life. Every day is full of ethical dilemmas, big and small, and it is as well to be aware of the fact. Whether we act in a good way depends in part on our ability to recognise the dilemmas, and in part on the ethical tools we have at our disposal.

Tools

Human beings are unique in many respects. No other animal has hands with such fantastic psychomotor skills, which have given us the capacity to create tools. No other animal has our brain capacity for communication, creativity and analytical thought. Human beings are also unique in that we have such a well-developed capacity to deal with ethical dilemmas. To help us, we have no fewer than five excellent ethical tools.

The first tool is that human beings have developed a succession of ethical principles, norms, rules and laws which indicate how we ought to act. They function as guiding lights. One principle concerns human value, and means that all human beings are of equal value. Another concerns the value of life, and means that we should protect life, and, as long as we can, try to maintain it. The autonomy principle, in turn, means that every individual has the right to make decisions about their own life. Another example is the principle of solidarity, which states that we should show solidarity and share what we have with those who have less.

These principles occasionally end up on a collision course with each other. An example of this is the question of abortion. On the one hand, the value-of-life principle says that the embryo has an innate value which is worth protecting. This value increases the further pregnancy progresses. On the other hand, the autonomy principle says that a person, in this case the prospective parent, has the right to make decisions affecting their own life. Legislators have solved this dilemma in Sweden by allowing the right of abortion until the eighteenth week of pregnancy, and in the UK by allowing abortion until the twenty-fourth week.

Examples of norms are that we should not lie, not speak ill of others, and that we should keep promises. These are conventions on which most societies agree. Breaking these conventions does not mean that we will be punished by society, but we may risk disapproval.

Breaking laws, on the other hand, can mean punishment by society. The legislation of human society can be traced from biblical times to our current advanced legal systems.

Principles, norms, rules and laws give us guidance, but they do not give us all the answers. If it were that easy, ethics would be a simple subject to deal with. Instead we need more tools in order to deal with the problems with which we are constantly confronted.

The second tool is our ability to reason, which helps us perform rational analysis and evaluate how we can do as much good as possible and how to avoid doing harm. The capacity to analyse the consequences of our actions is considerably more developed in human beings than in other species, and is something we can develop throughout our lives.

A hypothetical example: there are two collections going

on simultaneously at work. One is for a colleague who has cataracts and whose sight is getting progressively worse. Your colleague's problem is not advanced enough to qualify for an operation within the national health service, but must be performed privately. You are asked to contribute £100 towards the cost of the operation. The second collection is for people in Africa who suffer from an ocular disease that leads to blindness. You are asked to contribute £100, which is enough to save the sight of two people. You reckon you can only afford £100 in total. What do you do? Naturally we cannot solve this dilemma with reason alone, but it can contribute to the solution that we eventually reach.

There have been studies of the brain activity in people faced with two variants of a dilemma. In the first, you are standing on a railway platform and see a carriage rolling towards five people standing on the track. By pulling a lever you can switch the carriage on to another track, where another person is standing, who would be killed instead. Should you pull the lever? Most people say that they would do so.

In the second version, you can once again prevent the five men from being killed, but to do so you would have to push another person on to the track before the carriage reaches the five men. Should you do so? Most people say that they would not.

Even if the end result is the same, we react in different ways to these alternatives, partly because our action in the first only indirectly leads to a man being killed, whereas in the second we have to kill him directly, with our own hands.

The brain studies showed that when people took the decision to pull the lever, parts of the brain that are linked to reason became activated, whereas parts of the brain that are linked to emotion were activated when the decision to push someone on to the track was taken.

We have an inbuilt instinct not to kill which we must conquer emotionally if we are to be able to kill another human being with our own hands, whereas in the first instance we perform a rational analysis to determine how we should act to minimise the damage caused.

The third tool is our conscience, which acts like an inner compass and tells us what is good and what is evil. In the example of the railway carriage, it is primarily our conscience that we must grapple with when we have to decide whether to kill one man with our own hands in order to save five others.

Conscience functions as an emotional indicator of how we ought to act. These feelings of what is right and wrong have largely been instilled by the society in which we grew up. We construct internal values which often match those of the society around us. If we switch societies, or if society's values change, our own conscience's understanding of what is right or wrong can be affected. If we choose to act contrary to the voice of our conscience in a particular instance, this can also lead to us no longer regarding the action as wrong. We therefore silence our conscience. A similar thought is expressed in the Jewish scripture, the Talmud: 'Commit a sin twice and it will not seem to thee a crime.'

Our conscience should primarily be used as a tool before we make decisions, with the awareness that we will feel bad if we go against what our conscience tells us. We get a 'bad conscience' (which really is a strange expression, considering that the sensation it denotes does not indicate that our *conscience* is functioning in a poor way).

It is our conscience, or 'super-ego', which persuades us to take many fair decisions and stops us performing acts that would have negative consequences. Psychopaths lack this tool, but fortunately they are in the minority. Everyone else has access to this inner voice which can guide us. It is 'only' a matter of listening to it.

The fourth tool is our capacity for empathy – in other words, our ability to put ourselves in someone else's place. People simply do not think in the same way, have the same needs or the same expectations of the world around them. If we acted as if everyone had the same frame of reference, it would be wrong time after time precisely because we are all different. To know how we should act towards the person in front of us, we must first understand that person's needs. This is where our capacity for empathy comes in.

Empathy is not directly about doing good, but indicates an ability to understand how others think and respond. Then we can use this insight to do good – or not. Sympathy is about feeling *with* or *for* someone, whereas empathy is about feeling *as though we were inside* someone. Another way of expressing the difference is this: the purpose of sympathy is the well-being of the other person, whereas the primary purpose of empathy is understanding. The ability to think empathetically varies from person to person, but we all have the chance to develop this capacity during the course of our lives.

A common misconception is that it can be dangerous to feel too much empathy. It is said that we can wear ourselves out by taking on other people's suffering. But empathy is not about suffering in someone else's place, but about understanding our fellow human beings, and there are no indications that we can do ourselves harm by empathising too much. On the contrary, there are studies which show that a well-developed ability to empathise can protect us against burn-out, for instance.

The fifth tool is our fellow human beings, who we can use as a source of advice, and as sounding boards. Unfortunately this is a badly under-utilised resource in our society, because there is a widespread perception that we should manage on our own and not trouble others. Naturally, this is faulty thinking, because both parties win when one asks the other for advice. The person who asks gets advice and the chance to air their thoughts to a fellow human being. The person whose advice is sought usually feels honoured to have been asked, and in return gets the chance to grow and develop in the exchange of thoughts with another person. Asking someone's advice shows that we trust them and have faith in them. Asking for advice is therefore a form of gift.

Using our fellow human beings as a tool to help us solve ethical problems can be part of a system. For instance, in some workplaces there are ethical forums, where colleagues discuss problems that have arisen, and therefore have the chance to ask others for advice. Another method is mentoring, where experienced colleagues can advise others. But discussions with our fellows can also be more informal: you seek out someone who has previous experience of a problem, or who has a reputation of being a thoughtful person.

Asking others for advice is a powerful tool, which when used can, for instance, lead to the realisation that we are surrounded by a great many wise people.

So there you have them – five excellent tools. If we are conscious of these tools and develop our ability to use them, we will have a good chance of dealing with all the ethical dilemmas with which we are constantly confronted. Where dilemmas are concerned, there are of course no clear answers. We may be inclined to use particular ethical tools, but in the end they cannot give us sure answers. A well-considered decision is generally based upon an evaluation made with the help of several tools simultaneously. And in a well-informed evaluation, we will probably not know which of the tools played the decisive role. In the end, our decision may be partially based upon our own intuition, an overriding tool where we act according to a sense of what feels right or wrong.

With ethical decisions – as with so much else we do – we become cleverer the more we practise. Just as with chess, tennis or knitting, we become more skilful the more we do it. And ethical thinking is something that we can practise. It is worth accepting the challenge, because we have a great responsibility to manage our relations with our fellows and with the world around us. In the end the responsibility rests upon each individual to make good decisions.

FALSE KINDNESS ...

'Kind' is, as we have seen, a word that does not have solely positive associations. Being kind is often linked to stupidity, feebleness or weakness. As I have already indicated, I disagree with this, because to me being kind means something which is good, and, moreover, a form of intelligence. But I believe it is important to define what we mean by 'being kind', by differentiating it from qualities that can be misinterpreted as kindness – qualities that involve such elements as a lack of intelligence, weakness, manipulation and a lack of integrity. I call this 'false kindness', and, once again, I want to stress how important it is to discern genuine kindness from false.

False kindness as an inability to say no

A friend of my family had a daughter who was married to an alcoholic. The daughter was a lovely, considerate person who was regularly physically abused by her husband. Our friend was extremely worried about her daughter and her children. She used to relate their conversations, and tell us how she had tried to persuade her daughter to leave her husband, but the answer was always the same: that the husband would not be able to manage without her, and that it was important to keep the family together. One day our friend phoned us, utterly distraught. The man had killed her daughter in an alcoholic rage.

The daughter's intention had been to do good, but the consequences were the very opposite. She died, her husband ended up in prison, and the children lost both their parents.

Quite often we hide behind the excuse of kindness in order to act in a negative, or occasionally destructive, way. It becomes a shield of goodness which we can hold up in front of us. I do not know the true reasons why the daughter did not leave her husband. Perhaps it was exactly as she said. Perhaps her decision was also motivated by such factors as a fear of change, insecurity, loneliness, or a tendency towards self-destruction. The result was an act of false kindness with fatal consequences.

Genuine kindness means having the courage to stand up for what is right. And to speak up when something is wrong or wicked. Sometimes we see examples of false goodness in politics which can have terrifying consequences.

In 1938 Neville Chamberlain thought he was doing good when he reached an agreement with Adolf Hitler which he hoped would secure peace. With the benefit of hindsight we can see this as false goodness. Naturally it was not so easy to realise then what terrible plans Hitler had for the world, but the warning signs were there.

During the Second World War Swedish foreign policy was primarily concerned with keeping the country outside the war. Many other considerations were of secondary importance. This aim can naturally be regarded as honourable: to protect the population from war and possible occupation. One consequence of this strategy was that Sweden sold iron-ore to Germany, which was then used to produce weapons and other military equipment. Today those Swedish exports are regarded as having played a significant part in keeping the German war industry functioning so well, and for so long. This may have helped prolong the war, with all the consequences this had for a continuing loss of life. The protection of the Swedish people may therefore have had negative consequences for the rest of the world.

An experiment conducted by Stanley Milgram in the 1960s is now regarded as a classic of its kind. The participants were instructed to put questions to volunteers. If they answered incorrectly, the participants were to give them electric shocks of increasing severity (although there were never any electric shocks – the volunteers had been told to simulate pain). The experiment showed that approximately two-thirds of the participants were willing to give electric shocks which they believed were extremely painful.

The willingness to administer electric shocks was influenced by how active the participants needed to be in delivering them. Almost all acquiesced to these 'punishments' if they themselves did not have to press the button. About 30 per cent went so far as to be prepared to place the volunteer's hand on the plate that would transmit the shock. Another interesting observation was that if several people taking part in the experiment had been instructed to refuse to administer the shocks, then the subject of the experiment also refused.

In a similar way, totalitarian regimes can get people to commit atrocities by persuading them that they merely have to obey orders and not question anything. People can be convinced not to give expression to their own will, but merely accept others' truths as their own. One example are the crimes against humanity that were committed by Reserve Battalion 101 during the Second World War.

Reserve Battalion 101 consisted of 'ordinary men' from Hamburg who were too old to be called up for military service. They were not professional soldiers, nor were they specially trained by the SS. Despite this, the battalion's men played an active role in the Holocaust. They themselves killed approximately 38,000 people, and sent another 45,000 to the concentration camp at Treblinka. Strangely, the men were not forced to obey orders, and those who refused to take part did not suffer any reprisals. These crimes against humanity were therefore not committed under duress, but for completely different reasons, such as peer pressure and a desire to be cooperative, for instance.

Another example is the genocide in Rwanda in 1994, when civilian Hutus indiscriminately killed almost a million Tutsis and moderate Hutus (the latest official figure is 930,000). The victims might have been the neighbours or relatives of the perpetrators, and the murders were often committed with axes and machetes. Men, women, children and old people were mercilessly killed by 'ordinary people'. People fled to the churches, amongst other places, only to discover that they gave no protection. If the priests did not participate in the killing, they stood by passively. While all of this was going on, the rest of the world looked on.

Not to take a stand can sometimes be as great a crime as the crime itself. We must all have the courage to stand up for what is right when our fellow human beings are suffering. In the words of the historian Yehuda Bauer: 'We are all potential victims, potential culprits, potential observers.'

In the early 1990s I spent six months working at an infectious diseases clinic in Stockholm. On my first day there the doctors had gathered for a planning meeting when the door suddenly opened and one of the senior physicians walked in, very upset. He said that he had just had a phone call from a private clinic in Stockholm where an operation had been performed on a Greek woman.

She had developed blood poisoning and needed to be admitted to the intensive-care ward of our hospital. The only problem was that the woman was not a Swedish citizen, nor did she have valid insurance. Intensive care would be expensive, and who would pay? 'They want the cost to be paid from our clinic's budget,' the senior physician said indignantly. 'But I naturally said that if that was the case then we wouldn't take the woman.' Everyone around me sat silent. Some nodded, others sat there motionless. It was as though I had been struck by lightning, and I thought: We surely can't just let her die because we don't know who's going to pay? I wanted to say as much, but was I prepared to look like a troublemaker on my first day in the job? A few seconds passed while I thought about it. Then the door opened and a second senior physician walked in, explaining that he had heard about the case and that of course we would be admitting the woman. We would have to deal with the financial details later.

I was extremely ashamed afterwards, and have thought about those moments of doubt many times since then. I believe I would have objected if I had had a few more seconds to think, but I cannot be sure. I never actually took the chance to prove to myself that I dared. 'We are all potential victims, potential culprits, potential observers.'

An inability to act and make a stand can clearly be misinterpreted as a form of 'kindness'. Real kindness is something completely different. It is often about doing what we believe to be in the long-term best interests of another person. It is about sometimes making decisions which can in the short term look heartless. It can even be about acting in a way that will be condemned by those around us, because we are convinced that what we are doing will eventually have positive consequences.

False kindness masquerading as goodness

What appears at first sight to be good can turn out to be an expression of something completely different. What we initially perceive as kindness can hide other motives.

Many years ago I had a colleague who often expressed lofty morals. He did not hesitate to accuse others of scientific cheating. He gave his opinion when he heard pronouncements that he thought were morally unacceptable. On one occasion he accused a colleague of intentionally ruining his experiment, and declared this person evil. He was also careful to point out that he always told the truth, and that he expected the same thing from those around him, who, in his opinion, did not fulfil the same moral obligations.

Some time after he had left his job with us he asked me for summer employment, which he was given. When I returned from my holiday and found out that he had not been at work at all, I confronted him. He replied that he felt he had received such a low wage previously that it was no more than right that he should be compensated in this way. Before he vanished for good from our workplace, he used a grant he had been given for research to buy a computer for his own use, and claimed that this was his moral right when you considered how hard he had worked. When he later got divorced he cut his hours to part-time in order to avoid having to pay a large sum in child maintenance for his daughter.

Occasionally we come across people who suffer from so-called White Knight Syndrome. They seem to behave extremely kindly and considerately, until we realise that there is also a completely different side to them. If we are not alert, this can take a very long time. The problem is that they are often not aware of their own wickedness. This is because they lack the ability to integrate their own bad sides into their personality, but instead project them on to the world around them, which they then perceive as evil, while they themselves are pure as the driven snow – the knight in shining white armour.

When one of my friends had a child, she told me that she had decided never to get angry with the child. She had herself grown up with parents who had shouted at her constantly, and she did not want to subject her child to the same negative experience. And, to be sure, every time I saw them together she appeared to be friendly and tolerant, despite the fact that the child sometimes behaved very badly.

Until one day when the child was three years old or so. Almost the instant I set foot in their home I noticed the difference. The boy had smashed a vase on purpose, and his mother had responded by really shouting at him. I asked what was the reason for the change, and she told me that a few days before her son had behaved very badly, and that she had tried to talk him round in her usual way. He had looked at her and said: 'Mum, why is your mouth so pinched when you talk to me?' She had suddenly realised what was happening. She might be as angry with him as her parents had been with her, but it was just that she never showed it – or so she thought. The child had seen through his mother and recognised the anger beneath the mask of friendliness.

This phenomenon is usually called passive aggression. My friend had realised that it was better to express the anger which up to then had been bubbling under the surface, rather than to send the child mixed messages. She drew the right conclusions when she finally realised. Not everyone comes to this realisation, and as a result risks developing a passive aggressive lifestyle.

You are bound to have met someone like this. They are always friendly, they talk with a gentle voice, smile a lot. But at the same time you have an uncomfortable feeling that something is not right – a slight feeling of aggression, an intimation that they might not wish you well. And you are probably right – you have met someone who is passive aggressive.

Passive aggressive people cover their anger with a layer of friendliness, which gives them greater room for manoeuvre. Where openly aggressive people are concerned, there is no doubt when they are trying to get at us, which gives us a good chance of planning our defence. Passive aggressive people may wish us as much harm as openly aggressive people, but they are considerably more devious. We are not always as well prepared for the poisoned darts that they shoot.

False goodness can also be found within organisations. Charitable organisations where most of the income disappears into the founder's pockets are one example. These are organisations which have been established behind a false façade of goodness, where the founders themselves can continue to believe that they are doing good – 'Yes, but some of the money still gets through.'

Another example is communist regimes. The original communist idea was to topple an unfair and evil social system and create a utopian paradise on earth, where people could live in justice and equality. But in those states where the communists took power, things have largely gone very wrong. With the long-term goal of creating something good, the exact opposite has been created: a society without freedom, built on fear and oppression and with an excess of suffering. According to some estimates, more than 100 million people have been killed by communist regimes. As the British historian Christopher Dawson puts it: 'As soon as men decide that all means are permitted to fight an evil, then their good becomes indistinguishable from the evil that they set out to destroy.'

But there are also organisations that are founded with

the express intention of doing good, but where things nonetheless end up going wrong. The United Nations was created after the Second World War with the aim of securing peace in the world, if necessary with military means. In the UN constitution, article 43 includes the phrase: 'All Members of the United Nations, in order to contribute to the maintenance of international peace and security, undertake to make available to the Security Council, on its call and in accordance with a special agreement or agreements, armed forces, assistance, and facilities, including rights of passage, necessary for the purpose of maintaining international peace and security.'

This sounds very impressive. But how has it turned out in reality? Here are a few examples:

- During a three-month period in the spring of 1994, 930,000 people were killed in Rwanda in a murderous orgy organised by extremist Hutus. Despite the UN having military personnel in place inside the country, the organisation remained as good as passive during this genocide, which was eventually ended when Rwanda was invaded by Tutsi guerrillas from Uganda.
- In 1993, the Muslims in the Bosnian town of Srebrenica agreed to lay down their weapons in return for a UN promise of protection from attack from the Bosnian Serb militia. In 1995 the Bosnian Serbs attacked Srebrenica and took the Muslims prisoner. The women and children were sent away, and then a massacre began, in which more than 7,000 unarmed Muslim men were killed. What did

the UN do? The 600 UN soldiers from the Netherlands who had been stationed in Srebrenica with the task of protecting the Muslims were withdrawn, and the UN remained passive.

- In early 2003, fighting broke out between the black and the Arab population in the Darfur region of Sudan. The conflict has escalated into ethnic cleansing and what many regard as genocide. Over two million people, mainly black Africans, had become refugees by early 2006, and it is estimated that between 200,000 and 450,000 people have died. There are reports of rape, robbery, murder and widespread devastation, and in the refugee camps people are dying of disease and starvation. The UN has given humanitarian aid and imposed limited sanctions against the Sudanese government, but has otherwise remained passive, in spite of the risk of the situation growing even worse.

A global organisation which is intended to work for peace and freedom, and which does not fulfil its obligations, can in some respects be regarded as counteracting its own aims. A UN which is hamstrung by its own organisational structure when it is really needed is not only a problem for itself but for the whole world. The UN is one of our most important organisations, and it does much that is good, but unfortunately the organisation functions in a less than ideal way. Perhaps only true democracies ought to be permitted to join the UN, and all dictatorships, non-democratic communist states, repressive regimes and so on be left outside until they have become functioning democracies with freedom and human rights.

The concept of 'ingratiation' – meaning that you are exaggeratedly polite and friendly in the hope of gaining advantage – does not have terribly positive associations. Other similarly negative words are 'smarminess' and 'flattery'. These words are perceived as negative because they conjure up images of how a gullible person can be manipulated. We do not wish to be gullible, nor do we wish to be manipulated.

What should we think about these characteristics? Is it acceptable for people to act in their own interests under a mask of goodness? It all depends, in my opinion, on the probable consequences of the individual actions.

Naturally, it would be ideal if people always did good, and did so only for altruistic reasons, but seeing as this is not the case, at least not outside of fairy tales, we ought generally to be positive about people doing good things, even if their motivation is only to make a good impression. But when ingratiation is part of a broader plan for something that is not good, the action ought to be seen as negative. And it can certainly be difficult emotionally to put up with fawning people. The conclusion is that ingratiation and flattery can be both negative and positive. As so often where goodness is concerned, every case must be evaluated on its own merits.

★

Finally – hypocrisy aims to persuade people that a certain person is thoroughly good. Everything he or she does seems so noble and good that we mere mortals are embarrassed at our constant failure to attain the same high standards. At the same time, these people get on our nerves. The reason for this is that so few people are thoroughly good, and we generally have the capacity to differentiate between genuine and false goodness. Hypocrisy is a thin layer that we can usually see through.

Kind and stupid

In the common perception of kindness, there is often a link between kindness and stupidity. In fact there is no association between true kindness and stupidity. But there is also false kindness, which by its very nature is really stupid.

When our son was eight years old he managed to nag his way to being allowed to ride his bike around the suburb where we live. 'Everyone else in the class is allowed,' he asserted firmly. Eventually we gave in and let him ride his bike around on his own. I was worried about the decision but still thought it right, bearing in mind his integrity towards his friends and us. The following Saturday I was at home on my own when I heard the outside door open and close. Usually this was followed by a 'hello' which let us know who it was who had come home, but this time there was silence. I went downstairs and found my son racked with tears. I asked what had happened, and he told me, still sobbing, that he had been hit by a car. It had luckily managed to brake sharply before it hit him. He had only received a few scratches, but had been badly frightened. We agreed immediately that he would stop riding his bike without us until we all felt that he was up to it. Naturally, I blamed myself for wanting to appear kind and empathetic when our son had nagged us about riding his bike.

Who does not want to be a kind parent? We had walked into the trap of trying to seem good in a position where we should have been responsible adults and said no. Sometimes we have to do things which are perceived as mean by our child, because it is part of our task to show judgement. And this is a central aspect of raising a child – to act in a way which may sometimes make us unpopular in the short term, in the hope that everyone will benefit in the future. This is a typical example of false kindness which has its basis in an act of stupidity that could have had fatal consequences.

When Thabo Mbeki took over from Nelson Mandela as President of South Africa, the country was on the brink of a health-care catastrophe. More and more people were becoming ill with AIDS, and large parts of the population were infected by the HIV virus that causes the disease. What was needed was a huge information campaign, medicines to treat pregnant women who were HIV-positive to prevent their children being infected, actions to curb the spread of prostitution, and so on.

What did Mbeki do? He claimed that there was no proof that HIV was the cause of AIDS, and that the disease was instead linked to poverty. On several occasions he stressed that he had no intention of falling for thinly supported scientific theories about the causes of AIDS. He went on to claim that there were unspecified risks from taking the drugs that could slow the development of the disease and hinder its spread, which led to very limited use of these drugs in South Africa. During this period millions of people were infected with the deadly virus, many of them children. The South African population had to pay, and is still paying, a high price for Mbeki's personal theories about HIV and AIDS, which in the end are just a matter of poorly concealed stupidity.

The question of treating one's fellows well is a form of intelligence. We all have a fairly well developed ethical intelligence, and there is really nothing to prevent us from developing this ability during the course of our lives. 'Kindness', as I see it, is never linked to stupidity, but to good judgement.

To sum up

Being weak should not be confused with the idea of kindness. An inability to say no or to defend ourselves and those around us does not help anyone, and the end result will be negative. Nor is an inability to analyse adequately the results of our actions an expression of kindness.

Pretending to be kind, but really having other intentions, is not only thoughtless, but can also be risky.

Ethics can set sail under the false flag of kindness at the same time as our actions are really an expression of weakness, wickedness or sheer stupidity. It is important that in our dealings with other people we learn to differentiate between genuine kindness and its false equivalent. But even more important is being able to define our actions to ourselves, so that we strive for consequences that, as far as possible, are good.

. . . AND TRUE

Enough about false kindness, enough about stupidity, weakness and passive aggression. Now on to the genuine article. What does it mean to be kind, and what are the qualities that mark out a kind person? How should we think and act in order to be good?

Kind thoughts and good deeds

Sometimes it is claimed that a good person should only think good thoughts. And it is true that negative feelings about our fellow human beings are not good, and that we ourselves suffer most from having them. But at the same time we have to realise that there is no such thing as a perfect person. It is an unreasonable demand that we should never think mean or wicked thoughts. And how easy is it in actual fact to control one's thoughts? Without training our consciousness, it is extremely difficult. We can control various things in our lives, but we generally cannot control our thoughts.

So forget the message that various religious leaders have tried to drum into us, about the wickedness of thinking evil thoughts. On the contrary, I believe that it would be good to be free of the guilty conscience we get as a result of thinking wicked thoughts. If we can let off steam by thinking bad thoughts, then perhaps we can reduce the need to put them into practice.

We have considerably greater control over our actions. The decision to commit a good deed is our own, and the motivation behind the deed is not the most important thing. What matters in the end is what we do.

A friend who is known for being a bit mean comes to your birthday party with a pathetic little present, something which, to cap it all, you already have. When she sees the disappointment in your eyes she quickly says that she had planned to get something really nice, but unfortunately they did not have it in the only shop she had time to go to. Then she smiles and says: 'But it's the thought that counts.'

'It's the thought that counts.' I am just as taken aback every time I hear that expression. People resist helping one another, and then claim that they had intended to do good, but something got in the way. It does not matter if it is a question of a postponed meeting, the housekeeping money that you've lost on a bet, a method of child-rearing that went wrong, or birthday presents that you did not have time to get. Don't buy that excuse! Because it is *not* the thought that counts – it is the deed. If the deed is good, then the reason for the deed is of secondary importance.

Let us not place impossible demands on ourselves. We should try to do what is good and not have a guilty conscience for the wicked thoughts that sometimes pop up. It is not good for us to think wicked thoughts, but there is something worse, which is doing bad deeds. What matters in the end is the way that we act. And a kind person is, when it comes down to it, a person who *does* good things for other people. As the American poet J. R. Lowell put it: 'All the beautiful sentiments in the world weigh less than a single lovely action.'

So let us exile 'It's the thought that counts' to the storeroom for stupid platitudes – phrases which at first glance seem wise and thoughtful, but which upon reflection turn out to be quite unwise.

But if it is deeds that count, how can we work out the consequences of our deeds? How do we know that the deed we are committing will turn out good in the end? The answer is that we cannot foresee all the consequences of our actions, because they are endless. Every person's life touches thousands of others, and what we do in relation to another person influences in turn how they act towards other people, and so on, in an ever increasing circle.

Once, in a town in the north of Sweden, a woman

came up to me when I had just finished giving a lecture on ethics in the workplace. She said that she wanted to thank me for saving her life. I must have looked confused, and she went on to explain that she had attended a lecture I had given on cancer some ten years earlier in the same town. When I had finished the lecture, I'd announced that people were welcome to come up to me afterwards with personal questions, because it was normal to be a bit anxious about your own health when you have heard a lecture on cancer. The woman had shown me a skin lesion. I had said that she should have it removed at once. When she hesitated, I had said that I insisted. A few weeks later she had been told that the skin lesion was a malignant melanoma, a form of skin cancer, which needed to be removed at once. So now she wanted to thank me for the fact that she had been cured of cancer.

If she had not attended that lecture on cancer ten years before, her life might well have been different, and this in turn would have affected the lives of those around her. I myself could not even remember the woman, or the advice I had given her. And if she had not come up to me after the lecture, I would never have known how I had affected her life and the lives of those around her.

I once had a conversation with a learned Jewish rabbi who has written several good books. We got on to the subject of what it was like to write books read by a lot of people, without knowing how they will react. He said: 'Writing a book is like firing a sub-machine gun in the dark. You have no idea of who is going to be hit.' I must admit that I was at first taken aback at the rather brutal, if well observed, form of words this wise man used.

This is not only true of writing books, or making radio and television programmes, or films, or writing articles, or giving lectures – media activities which reach many people. It can just as easily apply to short encounters with strangers – in restaurants, on the bus, on the street. These encounters can affect people in ways that we will never know.

Every day we make decisions that affect other people, and we never find out what most of the consequences of our actions are. Is this reason enough to throw up our hands and say that it does not matter what we do, because the consequences are in any case unimaginable? No, absolutely not. The conclusion we should draw is that we should strive to do as much good as we can, and go on in the hope that our deeds will have positive effects. The Greek fabler Aesop wrote more than 2,500 years ago something which still holds true today: 'No act of kindness, no matter how small, is ever wasted.'

Kindness and judgement

Kindness is not primarily about thinking good thoughts, but about doing good deeds. This is not to say that kindness does not require any thought. On the contrary, kindness demands that we use all of our powers of thought and our ethical intelligence. Without good judgement it is difficult, not to say impossible, to be kind.

Those philosophers who devote themselves to ethics have various theories about how human beings ought best to behave towards one another in order for ethics to function optimally. Simplified, we can say that there are two main schools of thought about how we should handle ethics. According to the so-called duty ethics, human beings should be steered by norms and rules. Certain principles apply, and human beings should adapt their behaviour accordingly. The idea is that we should be driven by a sense of duty towards this system of rules.

According to consequence ethics (or utilitarian ethics) it is the result that counts. Instead of following rigid principles and rules, we should strive for solutions which benefit as many people as possible. To put it simply, we can say that the greatest possible good for the greatest number of people is the desire of the consequence ethicists.

I have previously discussed a situation that serves to exemplify these two points of view towards ethics. A railway carriage is careering towards five people on a track. We can act so that the five are saved, but the consequence of our action is that another man dies.

The duty ethicists could rely on the principle that we should not kill, and reach the conclusion that they could not sacrifice another man's life. The consequence ethicists could, on the other hand, claim that it would be better for one to die than five, and therefore conclude that the best result would be reached if we were to kill a man.

It is not difficult to see the problem with each of these schools of thought. To follow rules and norms all too strictly leads to a lack of flexibility, which means that human beings do not take the responsibility that is sometimes required in complex situations. One of the problems of consequence ethics is to try to work out how great the total amount of good will be after each individual act. Both schools have a tendency to lead to absurdities if followed strictly.

A classic example is the question of whether one would kill one healthy person in order for this person's organs to save five sick people. One of the consequence ethicists' reasons why they would not advocate this is that it would lead to 'social unrest' if people were suddenly being executed left and right. For me it is impossible to imagine that this could ever be acceptable, even if there were no danger of unrest.

The truth lies somewhere between these two philosophical schools. We should think both in terms of norms and rules, and in terms of the benefit to the greatest number of people. This is what ethics is like – sometimes there are no simple solutions, and we have to use the tools at our disposal, and our good judgement. The art of being kind assumes that we are reflective and discerning individuals. And responsibility for our actions can never be taken away from us.

Kindness and courage

My mother spent much of the war in the Warsaw ghetto, from where practically all Jews were transported to extermination camps and killed. On one occasion my mother and grandmother were taken to the so-called *Umschlagplatz*, from where they would be transported to the gas chambers. My mother's elder brother, Rudek, had previously told them that if they found themselves in the queue for the train, they should stand as far back as possible. As they approached the train after a long wait, Rudek suddenly appeared beside the queue. He had stolen a cycle and put on a policeman's cap, and said in an authoritative voice: 'These two are free to go.' The German soldiers were not sure of what to do, but were then distracted by disquiet in the queue, and Rudek took hold of his sister and mother and led them towards the exit. Once there, he repeated that they were released and together they returned to the ghetto. Later on Rudek managed to get the two of them out of the ghetto, and also to escape himself. My mother and her brother eventually survived the war after being sheltered by a family until Warsaw was liberated.

Rudek never wanted to talk about the war and the heroism he had displayed. I remember that when our eldest son was born I thanked Rudek not only because he had saved my mother, but also me and my children. Rudek smiled, but said nothing. My mother believed that the real reason Rudek did not like to talk about the war and his own efforts was that he thought he had not done enough.

My uncle could just have thought of himself, and would then have had considerably better chances of surviving the war. He chose to take responsibility for his family and succeeded in saving my mother as well. I believe that Rudek did not consider that he had a choice, that he had to act in that way. But he did have a choice, and he chose to look after other people. Good ethical decisions sometimes require courage.

Another example of great courage related to the Holocaust is the case of the Swedish diplomat Raoul Wallenberg. By distributing Swedish passports to Jews who were to have been transported to concentration camps, Wallenberg saved thousands of lives, at great risk to his own. Wallenberg disappeared at the end of the war, and is reported to have died in a Soviet prison. By his actions Wallenberg not only saved lives directly. His deeds also function as a reminder of how much good a single person can achieve, and as an example to inspire others to have the courage to do what is right for people in peril.

Winston Churchill was a Member of Parliament in the 1930s when Hitler began the rearmament of the German war machine. Churchill realised what was happening, and began an intensive campaign to spread awareness of Hitler's plans, and to ensure Britain armed in readiness for the war which seemed likely to follow. For a number of years Churchill was openly mocked in Parliament, and called a warmonger. In 1940, when war had already broken out,

Churchill was appointed Prime Minister with responsibility for a war effort that contributed so much to the defeat of Germany.

Sometimes we need to choose a path that others believe to be wrong, for the sake of good. Sometimes we might be mocked and even persecuted for what we believe will benefit many.

One study in America looked at the fate of so-called 'whistle-blowers' – people who had sounded the alarm about something they believed to be unethical in their workplace. All had lost their jobs, more than half had been bullied by their workmates before that, and more than 80 per cent suffered a deterioration in physical and mental health. But what is perhaps even more interesting is that almost all of them were pleased with their decision to raise the alarm. Having had the courage to do what was right was the most important thing in the end.

Courage can also be a question of identifying good aims, and then trying to reach these ideals, in spite of the odds of success seeming small. At the end of the 1980s I and a colleague, Dr Karl-Henrik Robèrt, had produced for the Swedish Board for Health and Welfare an information programme about AIDS, consisting of a cassette and a folder of images and text. Karl-Henrik started talking about producing a similar information package about the environment, which was one of his passions. One day he called me, full of enthusiasm. He told me that he had got the idea to produce a package about environmental problems which would be distributed to every Swedish house-hold, 4.3 million in total, and that in conjunction with its launch there would be television programmes and opinion polls, amongst other things. The money for the whole project would be raised from sponsors. A mad idea, I thought, but I promised to help, because if anyone could do this, it was Karl-Henrik, who possesses a unique com-bination of determination, creativity and courage. Less than a year later the whole project was completed, with the mailshot, television programmes and everything. It was the start of a period of intensive work involving research into environmental issues, the education of the authorities and businesses, and so on. The Natural Step foundation is today a successful environmental organisa-tion with offices in twelve countries.

Karl-Henrik was driven by a strong desire to contribute towards a better world. He had an inner belief which was transformed into action in a passionate way. A wish to do good, together with a large amount of courage, was enough to bring off this 'impossible' project successfully.

But courage need not always be about large projects, or about life and death decisions. Sometimes we need courage to act in more commonplace situations. A new person has been employed where you work. Soon you all discover that he has such bad body odour that everyone avoids going near him. Someone has raised the matter with your boss, who laughed in an embarrassed way and said that it is up to the employee how often he showers.

None of your colleagues seems inclined to act. Would you choose to say something to him in this instance?

I have asked this same question at many lectures, and always get roughly the same reply. A few of the participants say they would talk to their colleague, but the rest refrain, often with the motivation that it is not their business and that it would be embarrassing.

In the short term it does not seem especially kind to tell someone that he or she has bad BO. We can also ask ourselves whether this falls within the range of individual responsibility. You hardly know the person. And what if he gets angry?

What would happen to this man if no one makes him aware of his problem, and of the reason why no one seems interested in spending time with him? It is not unlikely that he will become isolated socially, eventually losing his job and moving on to another workplace, where the same problem would arise. And what about his private life?

From this perspective, the decision to intervene seems like a good deed, an expression of genuine kindness. But it is not easy, because it goes against the grain to say something like that to someone we hardly know. What is required for us to take that step? Courage – daring to stand up for your fellow human being – in spite of the fact that it might be uncomfortable.

In a study people were asked to determine which of two lines was longest. People who did the task alone answered correctly in 99 per cent of cases. But when they did the exercise in groups of five people – and the first four to answer had secretly been told to give the wrong answer – the subject answered incorrectly in more than one-third of instances. Evidently it takes courage and integrity to stand up to peer pressure.

It is not always the case that the majority is right and the minority wrong. Sometimes we might be alone in being right, while everyone else is wrong. Then it takes a great deal of courage to stand up for what is good. We must overcome our fear. As novelist and children's author Tove Jansson so wisely wrote: 'There is no problem being brave if one is not afraid.' It is when we are afraid that we are tested.

Sometimes norms, rules and laws are not enough

According to Swedish laws governing healthcare, hospital staff have an obligation of confidentiality towards their patients. There are a few exceptions, such as cases of certain infectious diseases, or if the patient has committed a crime that is punishable with at least two years in prison. Otherwise we are bound by an oath of confidentiality not to say anything about our patient.

Modern gene technology has made it possible to determine whether someone has a predisposition for certain inherited cancers. When a person has such a predisposition, there is often a 50 per cent chance that their children and siblings carry the same predisposition. For those who have this predisposition, there is generally a great risk that they will develop cancer, sometimes when they are young.

Imagine now that you are the doctor, and you are treating a woman for breast cancer. It turns out that this woman carries the predisposition for breast cancer, but she refuses to tell her younger sister, with whom she has not had any contact for several years, that she in turn has a 50 per cent chance of carrying the same predisposition (sisters like this are fortunately extremely rare). If the younger sister does not get this information, she is at real risk of becoming seriously ill, possibly at a young age. If you tell the younger sister, the chances of preventing the illness are considerably greater, but you would then be breaking the law and risk being reported to, and condemned by, the disciplinary board (not to mention causing the older sister to be furious with you). What should you do in this situation?

We have laws and rules because they should be followed. Otherwise we risk complete chaos. But sometimes we end up in situations where laws and rules are not enough, where society's norms do not match the reality. These situations are unusual, but they do occur. When we are confronted with these dilemmas, we have to face ourselves and we have to act as judge to our own decision. When society's ethics are not enough, we have to appeal to a higher form of ethics. I am not claiming that the example above is a situation where we should break the law. I merely mean that this might be such an instance.

When I present this dilemma to hospital staff, most say that they would follow the law and not tell the sister. Personally I have reached the conclusion, after a lot of thought, that I would tell the sister. One of the reasons is selfish. I do not want to meet the sister in a few years' time and know that I could have prevented the breast cancer that she could then be suffering from.

The phrase 'honesty is the best policy' is commonplace. It is a norm that suggests that at all stages of our lives we should be honest towards those around us, and towards ourselves. But is it so simple? Or is honesty a relative norm?

The psychoanalyst Ludvig Igra talks in his book *Den tunna hinnan mellan omsorg och grymhet* (*The Thin Line Between Care and Malice*) about an event that occurred during his early years. When Ludvig was just a few months old his parents left him for a while with a woman who lived in a house in the Tatra mountains in Poland. A riot broke out in the town, and people started running from house to house, searching for Jewish children, which they then killed. The woman swore that Ludvig was a Christian Polish child, and succeeded finally in persuading the men, who left the house. Ludvig states that his life was saved – by a humane lie.

This is an example of how goodness can find expression in a lie. But is it only in dangerous situations that we have the right to lie? Hardly. A little girl comes up to you, shows you a drawing and tells you proudly that it is a picture of a cat. Do you tell her that it looks more like an exploding fridge?

A close friend wonders what you think of her new coat, which looks like it comes straight from a horror film. Do you tell her?

You are having dinner with some friends, and have just managed to get through the piece of old shoe-leather you have been served when they ask what you thought of the meat. What do you say?

Tests have shown that the average person lies many times each day. One investigation revealed that 94 per cent of women questioned said that they lied regularly (men were not part of this investigation). Something they often lied about was their own weight (51 per cent), while 21 per cent lied about their income. Evidently different forms of lie are extremely common. And that is just as well. Because honesty is not always synonymous with being kind.

We have all met people who proudly proclaim 'I always say what I mean' or 'I always tell the truth'. Such utterances are warning signals. Because anyone who chooses always to be honest is abdicating from their responsibility as a fellow human being. They make it easy for themselves, because they have a fixed norm with which to arrange their lives, whilst the world around them is entirely unprotected from the truth-teller. Life is sadly not so uncomplicated that we should in all circumstances say what we think, or how things really are. Honesty, towards both ourselves and others, is an ideal worth striving for, but telling the truth can also be a weapon in the hands of someone who is not kind.

It may seem that all of the above justifies civil disobedience in all situations – that we have the right to act according to conscience when we believe something in society is wrong. This is not the case. This higher form of ethics demands great responsibility and good judgement. When I worked as a guest researcher in the USA during the 1980s, some animal-rights activists broke into the research institute's animal department and released as many animals as they could find. The problem was that some of the research being carried out in the institute was on rabies, and the activists also released dogs carrying the infection.

Only after great ethical tribulations ought we to go against the principles that apply in our society. We have laws, rules and norms for the reason that a society cannot exist without them. In principle they ought to be followed. But ethics sometimes places higher demands on us than these. A kind person is sometimes forced to do the right thing by 'doing wrong'.

Concluding, here is one more example of what can happen when people live according to rigid ethics and follow rules, norms and laws without giving much thought as to whether they are relevant. Three weeks after our second child was born, my wife and I decided to go to the cinema. My parents babysat our eldest son, and we took the baby into town to see the film *Awakenings* starring Robert De Niro and Robin Williams. We walked into the foyer and I went up to the ticket office and asked for two tickets. The cashier looked at our son, who was in a pouch on his mother's stomach, and said: 'You can't take the baby into the cinema.' I said that he was a quiet baby, but promised that we would leave if he did start to cry. She looked at me in surprise and said: 'That's not why – this film is for adults only.' When I had recovered from the shock and gathered my thoughts, I realised that this would be an excellent opportunity to use my medical authority (which is otherwise not of much use). So I stood up straight and said authoritatively: 'I happen to be a doctor, and know that three-week-old children cannot focus their sight yet. He won't be able to see anything on the screen.' She looked at me with a little smile and said: 'But he can hear!' After thinking about this for a moment, I could not help replying: 'I am proud and happy that you have such high regard for our three-week-old son's intelligence, but do you really think he has already learned English?' We did not get into the cinema.

To my great joy I read in the paper a few years later about a parliamentary motion which included the following passage: 'Laws must have a basis in reality if they are to be credible and respected. It is high time to look again at the rules of the Cinema Office, so that parents on maternity and paternity leave can take babies in prams into adults-only films.' Sometimes you are amazed when redress comes many years later, and that in spite of everything there is an overarching wisdom in society which can lead to unreasonable norms and rules being corrected with the passage of time.

Being kind to oneself

But isn't it dangerous to go about just thinking of others? Do we not risk wearing ourselves out with our concern for our fellow human beings? Isn't our world already full of exhausted people who have cared too much and whose sense of responsibility has been far too great?

It is true that we must also be kind to ourselves. We have to take care of ourselves at least as much as our fellows. Because if we do not, and we wear ourselves out, we will not be able to look after those around us.

But there is also risk involved in thinking like this. I remember a conversation I had more than twenty years ago, with a woman I knew quite well. She told me that she had reached the conclusion that she had spent too much time and effort helping and supporting other people and now she could not manage it any more. From now on she would think more about herself. The remarkable thing was that this woman was one of the most self-obsessed and unhelpful people I have ever met.

Since then I have heard many people say that they have spent too much energy looking after other people, and that from now on they would have to start looking after themselves. I have become rather sceptical, because a pattern has emerged – these people have generally never cared terribly much for the happiness and welfare of others.

People sometimes tell me that other people have told them that they are 'too kind', and that they ought to start looking after themselves instead. I think it is this 'instead' that is the trap a lot of people fall into. It is not a matter of being kind to yourself *instead* of being kind towards others. One of the best ways of being kind to yourself is precisely by being kind to others. There is no opposition between being kind to others and looking after yourself.

Sometimes we find ourselves in situations where we feel we are being exploited. We believe that we are being asked for too much, without getting anything back. How should we deal with situations like this? I think we should try to do as much as we can for as long as possible, until we reach a limit where we sense that our feeling of being exploited risks gaining the upper hand and souring our relations with other people. When we end up in situations like this, we should act in such a way that our relationships with our fellows do not suffer.

We should not forget to look after ourselves. We are also human beings and deserve to be looked after in a good way by ourselves, as well as by others. But treating yourself well does not mean treating those around you worse, or vice versa. On the contrary, I believe that genuine generosity towards our fellows and towards ourselves does not steal energy, but instead generates more.

So what is kindness?

True kindness is a desire to do good and to put this desire into practice. The motivations for being kind may vary, and may well be egotistical, as long as consideration of our fellow human beings is there and the deed is good. And in the end it is not the thought but the deed that counts.

A discussion of kindness which ends up concluding that goodness is often egotistical may seem crass. We want to believe good of people, after all. So the question is whether genuine kindness exists, a kindness driven by unselfish motivations. Yes, we may sometimes meet 'genuinely and truly' kind people, often amongst 'quite ordinary people'. They emit a goodness which is hard not to notice. Naturally we can never be sure that in the hours of darkness they are not robbing banks and beating up pensioners, but it seems extremely unlikely. These people with their radiant souls do exist. They ought to be a protected species, not just because they are so unusual, but because the human race needs them.

Sometimes ethics requires courage. Sometimes kindness requires us to do something which others believe to be less than good. But kindness must also be paired with discernment if the end result is to be good. It is true that striving for kindness places great demands on people. But it is a challenge well worth taking on. When it comes down to it, we all want to live in accordance with our ideals. And the vast majority of people want to be good fellow human beings.

COUNTERFORCES

We want to be good, but sometimes we end up acting in ways that are incompatible with our own ideals. Why is this the case – why don't we live as we would like to? The truth is that we sometimes miss the chance to be kind because of counterforces. Counterforces are factors that hinder us from acting in the best possible way, despite our best intentions.

Here are some common examples of counterforces and ways in which we could overcome them. The list is not exhaustive, but merely picks up on some of the reasons why we sometimes miss chances. One important precondition for us to be able to develop our kind side is that we understand why we act as we do – that we gain better self-awareness. When we understand the reasons why we sometimes do not do good, we are in a better position to be able to change.

Lack of time and resources

We live in a high-pressure society. People are expected to handle work, studies, family, friends, leisure time and their own development simultaneously. And we should do all of this in a good way. It is therefore hardly surprising that we constantly find ourselves short of time. Here is one example.

You have arranged to leave work an hour early because you have promised your son that you will go and watch his football team play in a cup final. You are anxious to get there on time, because you missed the semi-final in which he scored two goals when you ended up working late. He was very disappointed with you afterwards. Just as you have switched off the computer and are getting up to leave, the door opens. It is your boss, who, with a wild look in his eyes, explains that a serious problem has arisen, and that there will be a crisis meeting in ten minutes. You are needed at the meeting, he says before shutting the door. You sit in front of your computer and stare vacantly into space before making your decision.

How do we solve the conflict between a longing for self-realisation and a need to create as good an environment as possible for our children to grow up in? What do we do when several of our friends need us, and we don't have enough time? How do we handle two projects at work when both have already taken far longer than they should have? How do we solve the problem of prioritising between different tasks, when no one has yet managed to be in two places at the same time, and when we generally can't even manage to do two things at the same time successfully?

The answer is that there is no easy answer. In the end it comes down to developing the ability to prioritise in as good a way as possible. And – so that we do not burn ourselves out – learning to live with the decisions we make without regret. A guilty conscience about a well-thought-out decision does no one any good.

A similar form of counterforce in our society is a shortage of resources, which might seem paradoxical when you consider that in many ways we are today living in a world of excess. But the higher the standard we reach, the higher the demands we set, sometimes justifiably so. One example from my own area is the shrinking resources given to healthcare. It seems unreasonable that people should have to wait several months to find out whether or not they have cancer. It does not seem compatible with a welfare society that people are forced to wait over a year to have a worn-out knee joint replaced.

Beyond this there is a further factor – the poor use of existing resources because of inadequate management. Today, for instance, the average doctor in Sweden sees fewer than three patients a day; thirty years ago each doctor would see on average three times as many patients. Today's doctors are forced to spend their time on administration, documentation, unnecessary meetings, computer journals that aren't up to scratch and so on. Resources are not enough – they must be utilised in a good way.

It is not only the health service that lacks resources. Should children have to attend schools with thirty pupils in each class, and where the teachers have little if any pedagogical education? Should old people have to go to bed at seven o'clock, because the resources to care for them are insufficient?

A pronounced lack of resources can have even more widespread consequences. In extreme circumstances, ethical thinking can capsize completely. One example is the East African Ik people, who were forced to exist on the brink of poverty when the establishment of new national boundaries after the Second World War led to them being moved to an inhospitable mountainous region. According to the anthropologist Colin Turnbull, the tribe lost its sense of cooperation, empathy and ethics. They stopped sharing food, and left old people and children to die. This was linked to an almost sadistic enjoyment of the suffering of others. Even if parts of Turnbull's description have been questioned by other anthropologists, this remains an example of ethical thinking being disregarded because of extremely difficult conditions.

But we cannot raise this problem without simultaneously stating that people in difficult circumstances can also do a great deal for one another. The psychiatrist Viktor Frankl, who spent three years in the concentration camp at Auschwitz, writes: 'We who lived in concentration camps can remember the men who walked through the huts comforting others, giving away their last piece of bread. They may have been few in number, but they offer sufficient proof that everything can be taken from a man but one thing: the last of the human freedoms – to choose one's attitude in any given set of circumstances, to choose one's own way.'

When the tsunami swamped Asian beaches on Boxing Day 2004, hundreds of thousands of people died. In the middle of all the horror, survivors among the tourists told of how well they had been cared for by Thai people who had themselves lost relatives. Difficult situations can weaken our inner ethics, but they can also strengthen them.

A lack of empathy

When I travelled to the USA in my mid-twenties to take part in a scientific conference, I took the opportunity to visit my eighty-year-old grandmother, who used to spend the winter in a Florida hotel. During the days that I was staying with her, I significantly reduced the average age of the hotel's occupants, which was almost entirely populated by pensioners. My grandmother was disappointed in me because my relationship with my girlfriend at the time, Gabriella, had recently ended, and Grandmother had set her heart on having great-grandchildren. Several times she told me to 'sort things out with Gabriella again'. One day, by the pool, she had brought along a camera to take a picture of me. At her request I stood up, and then she started giving directions: 'Take a step forward, no, actually – go back, no, not that far, stand next to that table.' During all of this, more and more pensioners gathered around us, eagerly watching me as I was ordered about. Time after time Grandmother took the chance to tell the growing crowd that I was her grandson from Sweden. I grew increasingly unhappy at my exposed position, but tried to put a brave face on it. Eventually she put the camera down, and said with a happy smile: 'Stefan, you look so unhappy. Do you know why? It's because you miss Gabriella!'

Empathy is the ability to understand another person's way of thinking. We all have this capacity, more or less well developed. Even my grandmother had empathetic abilities, although on this occasion she was blinded by her desire to make things right between me and my former girlfriend, and could not see the real reason for my unhappy appearance.

If we want to be kind to other people, we must also know how they want to be received, otherwise we are grasping in the dark. Our desire to do good can have negative consequences if there is a discrepancy between what we think a person wants and what they really want. The parent who does not let his or her child out to play with friends in the evenings because of his own anxiety. Colleagues who interpret someone's sudden withdrawn behaviour as a desire to be left alone and who do not realise that she was depressed until she has taken her life. The man who does not understand that his wife's anger is the result of her not feeling appreciated, and who finally moves out to get away from the arguments. The patient who does not want to seem difficult and says to the unsuspicious doctor: 'Oh yes, I'm fine,' and who then does not receive the correct treatment for his problem.

It is not easy to imagine another person's thoughts, especially considering that we do not always understand our own. We do not always know how we ourselves will react in a new situation. One example is relatives of patients with Huntington's disease.

Huntington's disease usually manifests itself between the ages of thirty and fifty, and it becomes a very serious illness. The patient gradually develops physical and mental symptoms, becomes increasingly incapacitated, and eventually dies of the disease. There is at present no treatment that leads to a cure. Huntington's disease is an inherited illness, and the children and siblings of sufferers carry a 50 per cent risk of also developing the disease. For some years now researchers have tried to come up with a test to determine at an earlier stage whether relatives of sufferers are likely to develop the disease. When a group of relatives was asked if they would like to take the test when it was available, 90 per cent said they would.

A few years ago the test was successfully developed. When the relatives were told that the test was available, only 50 per cent said they wanted to be tested. Eventually only 10–15 per cent took the test.

We do not know how we will react in a new situation. We may have some idea, but it is often wrong. And if a person does not know how he or she is going to react in a certain situation, it is clear that it is even more difficult to imagine how other people are likely to act and react.

People respond differently to different situations, people within the same society have different needs and wishes, and, on top of this, people from different cultures and societies experience one and the same situation in different ways.

Some years ago we held a course on cancer for a group of research students. Within the course there was to be a patient demonstration – a conversation between a doctor and a patient. During the break two Chinese doctors came up to us and wondered if we usually told our patients that they had cancer. When we said that we did, they were astonished, and said: 'But then you're killing them prematurely. We think you're being unethical!'

When doctors from certain other countries choose, instead of telling the patient they have cancer, to say that they are suffering from another less malign illness, it may be because they do not want to destroy the patient's joie de vivre, or even their desire to live, which is assumed will vanish as soon as they know they are suffering from a difficult and stigmatising disease. For us, though, this thought seems alien.

We have a tendency to believe that the set of ethics that applies in our culture is the only right one. This is of course not the case. We must keep an open mind to the fact that ethics often does not involve absolute truths.

Who are we to say that we are always right, and everyone else wrong?

In the late 1980s I met a woman at the hospital who had fled Romania some months before, and who was now seeking asylum in Sweden. She had left her eight-year-old daughter behind, but hoped to be reunited with her after a few years in Sweden. The woman told me that she had an inflammation of the chest which had been treated in Romania with radiation and chemotherapy, and now she was seeking treatment in Sweden because she thought the illness had got worse. Her doctor had referred her to the Department of Oncology. When I examined her, I found that she had a completely different diagnosis to what she had told me – breast cancer which had spread to the chest. I realised immediately that the disease was incurable, and that she would in all likelihood die of it. After considering the situation, I told her that she had cancer. The woman became distraught, but the very next day she was on a plane back to Romania and her daughter. Before she left, she wrote me a letter thanking me for telling her the truth, and expressing her anger at having had the correct diagnosis concealed from her before. If she had only known, she would never have left her daughter and wasted those months in a foreign country.

These examples describe the same phenomenon – that people experience different situations in different ways. There are no hard and fast rules governing how we should act – we must take what each new encounter throws at us and use our ability for empathetic thought. It is not easy to do the right thing for other people if we do not understand their way of thinking. And we should not imagine that it is easy to understand another person's inner world. But if we want to develop our kind side, one approach is to develop our empathy. However good or bad our empathetic abilities are today, we always have the chance to develop them if we decide it is important to do so.

Lack of reflection

A friend once told me that he usually lay awake for an hour before falling asleep, but that he didn't mind because it gave him the opportunity to think. 'What do you think about?' I asked.

'Well, during the day I think a lot about my work, so I set this time aside to think of good things I can do for my family.'

Far too often we make decisions that are lacking in kindness, not because we do not want to be good, but because we are thoughtless. We simply do not devote enough time and energy to analysing the situation to see how we could best act. Instead of utilising our ethical tools, we act without reflection. A lot of our decisions need not necessarily lack goodness, if we only thought about them more before acting.

The golden rule, which is found in many religions, says that we should treat other people as we ourselves would like to be treated. Even if I think that this has its short-comings (it would be better to treat others how *they* would like to be treated), the golden rule still has much to teach us. Much wiser decisions would be made if we thought: How would I want other people to treat me if I was in this situation?

The most important way of avoiding lack of reflection as a counterforce is, however, to decide to become more reflective. It is also important that we learn to differentiate between those situations in which we can act out of reflex, and those which demand reflection first.

My father said in several newspaper interviews that he had one regret about his life: not spending more time with his children when they were small. But then he added that if he could live his life again, he would prob-ably do the same thing again. I must admit that I have never really understood this statement, but I think he meant that the awareness that he had acted wrongly would not have changed his priorities. He would still have done the same thing, but after more reflection. The decision would have been taken on a more conscious level.

If we start to spend time analysing everyday ethical decisions, not only do the chances of us solving real prob-lems increase, but also it is an investment in the future, because we are also training our ability to think ethically – our ethical intelligence.

Not wanting to get involved

When my sister and I were small we had nannies – our parents both worked full-time and were away during the day. One of the nannies beat us. Our torment eventually came to an end when a neighbour told my mother that she had heard sounds of abuse coming from our flat. When my mother asked how long this had been going on, the neighbour replied embarrassed that she had heard it for a while, but had not wanted to get involved. It was not her business. She hoped my mother wouldn't think badly of her for getting involved now.

Awareness of the evil of child abuse is far more widespread now than it was during my childhood, but the example still indicates a general phenomenon. Is it our business if a colleague is feeling bad? Should we phone a friend who has lost someone dear to them, or do we persuade ourselves that she would rather not be disturbed? Should we get involved if we see a parent hit his child in the street? All too often people tell themselves that it is not their business.

Many of my cancer patients and their relatives have similar stories to tell. When knowledge of the cancer diagnosis has spread to friends and acquaintances, some people are there to give help and support. Others just disappear. A special variant of this, which many patients describe, is that people avoid them if they happen to bump into one another. 'I saw how they looked away and pretended not to have seen me' – I have heard that line many times.

When you ask people why they do not do what seems obvious – showing that they are there to help – they often reply that they do not 'want to get involved' or 'seem pushy'. There are probably other reasons for their actions, for instance being afraid of illness and death, or insecurity about how they should act, but, more or less consciously, the excuse used is usually that they do not want to intrude or interfere.

There is an inbuilt error in our society. Everyone is supposed to cope on their own. We ought not to disturb each other, and we should mind our own business. This is of course faulty thinking, because we live in a society where our dependence on others is immense – considerably greater than in earlier ages, when smaller groups could be more or less self-supporting. It would make sense to acknowledge our dependence on others, to accept the help we need, and give help when we are needed.

Next time you are wondering whether to mind your own business, ask yourself: If it isn't my business, whose is it? Whose task is it to be a fellow human being?

Not practising what we preach

When I give lectures, I often use examples in which the audience have to take a stance. In one of these I describe a situation where a colleague has an obvious problem with alcohol. Then I ask whether the audience would choose to act in order to help their colleague, or whether they would choose to do nothing. It never fails – more than 95 per cent of those asked say that they would help their colleague.

This is naturally a positive result. But there is one problem: how things are in reality. When you talk to sober alcoholics, a lot of them say the same thing, that practically everyone where they worked must have known about their alcohol problem, but that no one did anything.

This is an example of the difference between our internal norms – how we think we should act – and how we act in reality. And sometimes there is an abyss between how we *want* to live our lives, and how we actually choose to live.

Another example is an experiment carried out on students training to be priests. They were asked to go to a nearby building to give a lecture at short notice. On the way to the lecture they passed a man who was leaning forward and groaning (he had been placed there by the researchers). The majority of the trainees chose to ignore the troubled man, but a minority offered him their help. A particularly interesting aspect of this experiment is the subject of the lecture the trainees were asked to give. It was to be about the Good Samaritan, the story of a beaten man ignored on the roadside by several passersby – among them a priest – until he is finally helped by a Samaritan.

Naturally the results of this experiment may also depend on the counterforce of lack of time, because the more of a hurry the trainee priests were in to start the lecture, the less likely they were to help. But at the same time we cannot help but conclude that this is an example of failing to live as you preach.

There are even examples of the opposite, situations where a widespread norm does not hold in reality, and this is a good thing. We occasionally act in a better way in reality than in our thoughts. In one investigation, Swedes were asked if they consider animals and humans to be worth the same, and almost 50 per cent replied that they did. The result seems to indicate that many of us are great animal lovers and really care about animals.

But how does this work in reality? I have sat outside on many summer evenings with the air buzzing with mosquitoes, and seen how most of the people present do not hesitate to kill a large number of flies, whose only intention was to try to satisfy their hunger. And if a puppy and a baby fall in the water, would almost 50 per cent of Swedes really consider choosing to save the puppy? Surely not (which, however much I like cute little puppies, I happen to think is the right decision).

We want to live in unity with our ideals. So it is important to be conscious of the chasm that sometimes exists between our ethical norms and our actions in real life, because then we can do something about the discrepancy. We all want to live as we preach. But we must be conscious human beings in order to do so.

Our innate aggression

One day in December 1984 a man named Bernhard Goetz was travelling on the New York subway. In the same carriage was a group of four youths who, it turned out later, all had criminal records. When one of the youths, backed up by the others, threateningly approached Goetz and demanded five dollars, Goetz drew his pistol and shot all four of them. One of them was shot a second time, as he lay injured on the floor. When a conductor came up to him, Goetz said: 'I don't know why I did it. They were trying to rob me.' Then Goetz fled from the scene, but later gave himself up to the police. Goetz had had many conflicts with those around him, and existed in a state of express frustration at how society had developed, but, as far as we know, had never previously committed an act of violence. Interestingly, he was praised as a hero and was cleared in court.

In the 1970s Philip Zimbardo of Stanford University conducted an experiment which will probably never be repeated. Its purpose was to find an explanation to the fevered hatred in the country's prisons. Together with colleagues, he built a 'prison' in the cellar of the university, and advertised for people to take part in the experiment. Twenty-one people were selected by interview as being mentally stable. These were then divided into two groups: 'guards', who were to maintain order in the prison, and 'prisoners', who were to be guarded by the others. To mimic reality as closely as possible, the police were asked to assist by arresting the participants in their homes, taking them to the police station and then transporting them to the prison.

The guards' abuse of the prisoners began on the very first night, and grew steadily worse. Amongst other things, the prisoners had their clothes removed, were handcuffed, sprayed with fire extinguishers, and generally mistreated. After six days the experiment, which was to have run for two weeks, was stopped, after several of the prisoners had suffered breakdowns.

The experiment showed that ordinary people can become extremely aggressive under specific circumstances, and that this aggression can tip over into sadism. This does not just apply to 'other people' – we all harbour an innate aggression. We often control it in order to function in social contexts, but occasionally the lid is lifted and we act aggressively, sometimes in ways that surprise even us. Merely pretending that this trait does not exist can be counterproductive, and can, for instance, take expression in passive aggression. The important thing is that we accept this side of ourselves, so that we can control it. Otherwise the aggressive impulse can stop us from doing what is good.

Some time ago I spoke to a friend whose mother was seriously ill. His mother phoned him every day, asking for help with various things. Sometimes he reluctantly did what she wanted, but just as often he refused. When I asked why he did not help her, his face contorted in anger and he snarled: 'I needed her for years, but she never cared enough to help. My mother has always put her own needs before mine. But now that she needs me, she's happy to acknowledge me. Why should I be there for her when she never was for me?' He looked angrily at me. I replied: 'Perhaps because the last thing you want is to be like your mother.'

By nature human beings have an aggressive side. It has been an evolutionary advantage, and is one of the reasons why we have survived as a species. But this trait has also been to our detriment, both collectively and individually. The characteristic that allowed us to defeat threatening animals, hunt for food and create beneficial competition, which has hastened our development, has also been the great curse of humanity. In addition to war, intolerance, violence and murder, this trait also means that we feel anger, hatred, irritation and contempt towards our fellows, whom we sometimes do not even know. Just think of how drivers treat one another during the rush hour on Monday mornings.

Sometimes we choose not to be kind to other people because we feel aggression towards them. We may feel disappointed in them, not like them, be irritated by them, feel that they do not like us, and so on. Often we put the blame on them and decide it is the other person's fault that we feel the way we do. But the truth is that we resist the opportunity to do good because we cannot handle our feelings of anger, disappointment, irritation or loathing. It is no one else's decision, and no one else's fault, that we choose not to do good.

It is difficult to say to someone that they should stop being angry. Anger is an emotion over which we have no direct control. What we can do, though, is to choose not to act upon this emotion.

I myself am an example of someone who has had, and sometimes still has, a good deal of inner aggression. I was regarded as a difficult child, and during my early school years I was often involved in fights. I had a volatile temper and was quick to answer back when I felt offended. Over the years I have learned to control this impulse. The interesting thing is that as I have learned not to act upon my aggressive impulses, the aggression itself has decreased.

I am certainly not claiming that we should never get angry. When we live in close proximity to each other, as in a family unit, it is unavoidable that we should sometimes act out our anger and frustration. Studies of couples' relationships have shown that in principle there are three ways in which couples behave in conflicts. They either avoid confrontations entirely, have a listening and responsive attitude, or act out their anger in quarrels. It turns out that the third group is not necessarily the worst type of relationship. On the contrary, these relationships may be very loving, in between the quarrels. Studies of our closest relatives, the apes, have shown that conflicts within a group can be followed by tender scenes of reconciliation. The most important thing is perhaps not the fact that we quarrel, but how we do so, and whether we have the capacity to make up in a positive way afterwards.

Aggression is part of the human personality, and something we cannot avoid. Our task is to control and channel our aggression in a constructive way. And to be conscious of the fact that, in almost all instances, uncontrolled outbursts of aggression do damage to us ourselves.

It is up to each of us to decide if we are going to let aggressive feelings be a counterforce to our chances of doing good. However badly we may feel others have behaved towards us, whether they be our parents, colleagues or fellow commuters, it is up to each of us to decide if we are to be helpless victims of our feelings, or if we are going to be in control of our own lives. It is never the case that we are responsible for experiencing an emotion. But we may be responsible for having acted it out.

The victim mentality

'It's a terrible situation, but there's nothing I can do about it. I'm powerless.' How often do we convince ourselves that we are helpless victims? That there is nothing we can do about a particular situation? However willing we may be, we can see no way to improve things.

In the Zurich railway station stands an old woman. She has stood there every day for a decade. Heidi used to be a nurse, but now she is retired. She leans against her wheelchair and her crutch and looks tenderly at the travellers walking by. Day in and day out, sometimes fourteen hours a day. What on earth is she doing there? Well, she's blessing the travellers. She looks at them with love and gives them her blessing. Is she helping anyone? It depends on what each of us believes, but the important thing is that she tries. She does not see herself as a victim. She fights in a way she can, and in a way that she believes in.

Whenever I end up in a situation where I feel helpless, I sometimes think of the old woman in Zurich station. She tries to make a difference to her fellows, if only by giving them her loving blessing. If an old woman who cannot even stand without support can spend all her time trying to help others, surely there can be no limit to what you or I can achieve?

The excuses for not doing so are many.

'I know I ought to visit my aunt in hospital more often, but I just don't have time.'

'I'd like to give more money to charity, but I need some sort of nest egg for the future.'

'I'd like to have a more meaningful job, but then I'd lose the security of a regular income.'

'I'd like to help my colleague, but I can't handle more responsibility.'

'I'd really like there to be peace on earth, but what could I possibly do?'

In none of these instances are we helpless victims. We can all do something. For those close to us. For those we know. For those we work with. For all those we encounter. The truth is that we can contribute towards a better world.

A few years ago an interesting phenomenon arose at toll booths in the USA. When people arrived at the booth, they discovered that the motorist ahead of them had already paid for them. So they put in their money for the car behind them, and so on. This has developed into a movement where people do things for others without asking anything in return and without the recipient knowing who the donor is.

This is an example of people doing things for others, at little or no cost to themselves. The phenomenon itself makes people feel happy, instils a faith in mankind and a sense of reflection.

There is one occasion when patients tend to seek a second opinion or try alternative treatments. It is when the doctor says: 'There is nothing I can do for you.' This is not only bad psychology, it is also untrue. There is always something we can do. If we can no longer cure, then we can ease the suffering. If we cannot do that, we can comfort. And if we can no longer comfort, we can simply be there.

Evidently we sometimes fail to act because we believe that we are helpless. In this way the victim mentality becomes a counterforce, even though the truth is quite different – that we are never helpless victims. There is always something we can do for others.

The 'someone else' principle

The 'someone else' principle is a special term for the unwillingness to do a good deed. It means that you say to yourself: 'It isn't my responsibility. It's someone else's.' The 'someone else' principle is a remarkable variant of passivity, because it means that we expect someone else to do what we could actually do ourselves. One example was when a middle-aged man wearing shabby clothes had to lie on a pavement in Stockholm apparently unconscious for half an hour while hundreds of people walked past him. Presumably they were all thinking roughly the same thing as they passed: It isn't my responsibility. It's someone else's.

One day in 1964 Catherine Genovese was attacked by a man on her way home from work in New York. He chased her across a car park and when he finally caught her he stabbed her repeatedly with a knife. Her screams were heard by several neighbours, one of whom called out to the attacker to leave her alone. He left her in the street, bleeding badly. No one came to her aid, and a few minutes later the man returned and continued stabbing her with the knife. Once again, the neighbours heard her screams, but no one helped her or called the police. Once again the man disappeared, only to return to the still living woman a few minutes later. This time he assaulted her sexually, and took 49 dollars from her purse. Then he killed Catherine Genovese with further blows with the knife. In total she was stabbed seventeen times.

At a reconstruction of the murder it became apparent that during the thirty-two minutes over which the attack took place, thirty-eight people heard Catherine Genovese's calls for help or witnessed the attack. No one came to her aid or called the police. Some of them said they did not want to get involved, others said they thought someone else would already have made a call. Some just said they had been frightened, or could not be bothered.

Research has shown that our willingness to help decreases in relation to how many other people there are in the vicinity who could possibly help. In one experiment the participants sat in small rooms and were, via a telephone system, in contact with other people in neighbouring rooms. One of these people said that he occasionally suffered from seizures, and after a while said that he felt unwell and needed help. The experiment showed that in 85 per cent of cases people tried to help if they thought they were alone with the unwell man. If there was one other participant involved, the willingness fell to 62 per cent, and if there were four more participants, they only helped the man in 31 per cent of cases.

Another experiment looked at how many people would help a man who collapsed on an underground train. If the man was carrying a stick he was helped in 95 per cent of instances. If he had a bottle of liquor in his hand and smelled of alcohol, he was helped in only 50 per cent of instances, and after considerably longer time. Evidently the principle of people being of equal value does not always work in reality.

The 'someone else' principle is a dangerous counter-force, because it means that people act as though they have less responsibility than everyone else. This is not the case – we all have a responsibility towards our fellows, to be there for them. And if we do not realise this, the result may be that no one takes the responsibility that might have saved somebody's life.

Whatever we do, it'll turn out wrong

My dad told me about something that happened during the Second World War. Being Jewish, they had been taken to a concentration camp. My grandfather was a tailor, and his family was probably saved by the fact that the Germans made him sew clothes for them. One day my father was in the room that was used as his father's workshop. Grandfather was trying a pair of trousers on a German officer, who was accompanied by a colleague. While Grandfather was on his knees in front of the officer, one of the Germans asked: 'What do the Jews say — how will the war fare for the Germans?' My father was horrified, because he knew that Grandfather would not lie to the Germans. Would Grandfather instead choose to say what everyone believed — that the Germans would lose the war? The consequence of this might be that they would kill him.

Sometimes we end up in situations where whatever we do can be both right and wrong. All possible options seem to have both advantages and disadvantages. The situation in which my grandfather found himself is an example of just such an ethical dilemma.

In William Styron's book *Sophie's Choice*, the main character is faced with an impossible dilemma. She has been transported to Auschwitz with her two children, and is standing in front of an SS doctor who forces her to choose – one of her children will be sent for immediate execution, while the other will live, at least for a while. Under immense duress, Sophie makes her choice and one of the children is taken away. But Sophie can never reconcile herself to the decision she was forced to make, and this leads eventually to her demise.

'Impossible' ethical dilemmas are naturally rarely as dramatic as this example, but they are considerably more common than we might be tempted to believe. In my work as a ward physician, it was not uncommon at the end of the afternoon for me to have several patients left to see, all of whom needed to be spoken to in peace and quiet. Who should I prioritise before I had to leave?

Should we stay at home and help our children with their homework, or go and visit a good friend who is depressed? Should we give money to Save the Children, or buy a nice present for our partner's birthday? Should we help an old lady off the bus, or have time to make our connection in order to get to an important meeting? It may also be a question of when to break with norms and rules. Should we lie to protect a friend? Should we break a promise because we think it would benefit the person to whom we made the promise?

These situations sometimes lead to a feeling of negative stress. We feel bad because we can see no good solution, however hard we try. Too much negative stress can in turn lead to both mental and physical problems.

What should we do to be good in a situation where all

possible options are less than good? How can we do right in situations where all the options are more or less bad? The answer is that we must evaluate each situation on its own merits and then do our best.

There is a further response: sometimes there is a hidden door we can open. Let us return to my grandfather and see how he solved the dilemma in which he found himself. Grandfather sat silent for a long time. Eventually the second officer said sharply: 'Didn't you hear the question?' The Grandfather said in a low voice: 'Not only the Jews, but all the world knows that the Germany of Goethe and Schiller can never be eradicated.' The Germans looked at each other, bemused, and then started to talk about something else. By referring to the treasures of German culture, Grandfather had escaped from the situation without either lying or being shot. Wise – extremely wise.

How to handle counterforces

We are hindered from doing good in various ways by counterforces. In spite of our best intentions, things do not always turn out well. How do we then deal with counterforces? In the same way as all other problems – a precondition for being able to deal with them and finding a good solution is that we understand why we act in a specific way. Consequently we must be aware of when counterforces are involved. Once we know this, the problem is easier to handle. The decision can be taken on a more conscious level.

Another important aspect is that we take the decision that we really want to solve the problem. When we feel the fundamental driving force to achieve a change, that usually opens the door as if by magic. A third factor is that we sometimes have to deal with old ways of thinking. It may be that counterforces consist of a non-constructive way of reasoning, which we may have carried with us from childhood. Sometimes we find the solution by questioning old patterns of thought, and thinking in new ways instead.

DO WE BENEFIT FROM BEING KIND?

In the discussions after my lectures, I often hear people say that the world is an evil place. I personally do not perceive existence like that. My view is that the world is basically good, but that there is a widespread focus upon that which is bad or evil. To look at the news is enough to pick up the warped perception that most of what happens is bad. But on the other hand, where is the news value in the following?

- The Peterson family gains a third healthy child.
- Mrs Wilson, after falling and breaking her hip during a walk in the woods, is rescued by a skier who fortunately had decided to take an evening ski.
- After a lot of hard work, Michael Stephens has got into the university course he wanted.
- Mr Patel's son has paid back his bank loan which

means that his father will no longer have to lose his flat and move to an old people's home in another town.

It is hardly surprising that we get a distorted view of reality when the focus is so often upon all that is negative in life. We may be upset that people are beaten up on the underground. But we can also be amazed that, in the crush that occurs during rush-hour, the vast majority of people manage to cooperate and be friendly towards one another *without* ending up in fights. Many other species would never manage to be in such close proximity without constant outbreaks of violence.

My belief is that the vast majority of people wish for the well-being of others in the vast majority of situations. If you spend a day watching the people around you, this becomes evident. People speak to each other in a friendly way, they help each other when accidents happen, they intervene when they see something happening that they perceive as wrong. Of course we may see examples of the opposite. Every person is capable of good and bad actions. But the bad and malicious deeds are considerably less common than the good ones.

There is also a widespread belief that ruthless and self-centred people are the most successful when it comes to their careers. Being prepared to do anything to get ahead is perhaps not a positive characteristic in everyday life, but when it comes to work, this trait may suddenly be seen as an advantage. If you are merely sufficiently hard and ruthless, and lacking in conscience, then your career will be a sure-fire success.

In this scenario, the kind person is often placed in sharp contrast to the thoughtless egotist. The kind person is a wimp who is constantly deceived and flattened by the self-obsessed bully. The kind person's nice perceptions of how people should act are crushed by their ruthless colleague's razor-sharp arguments. The kind person ends up the loser, but is fortunately too unintelligent to realise this obvious fact – instead they lick their wounds, and persist in their pathetic and rather dumb kindness. It is not so surprising that Hollywood producers have made fortunes from films in which the simple-minded, wimpy but kind person finally, against all expectations, gets their revenge.

Is this an accurate picture of reality? Hardly. It needs to be repeated that it is kindness that wins in the long run. Kindness is a form of intelligence that pays dividends, while someone who is not kind misses out on considerably more than just a visit from Santa Claus once a year.

But it is a natural question – why should we really be kind? Can we not have just as good a life if we are self-obsessed, mean and unkind? Are there any statistics which show that people who are caring and good-hearted are less afflicted by cancer, accidents, chronic diseases or divorce?

Unfortunately no such statistics exist as yet. Instead, what follows is a number of observations which support the conclusion that we have a lot to gain by being kind. Some of these conclusions are based upon scientific studies, where-as others come from empirical observation.

Studies of animals

Mankind is a herd animal, like a lot of other species. This means that we do not simply look after ourselves, but also act for the survival of the group. The welfare and survival of the individual is enhanced by the welfare and survival of the group. Alone is not strong. Originally, during the time when we were nomads, this feeling of belonging was largely confined to members of the same group or tribe. As better communications have been developed, and human society has become more organised, the more we have expanded this feeling of group-belonging to include increasing numbers of people.

We may ask ourselves how much our sense of con-tributing to the welfare of the collective has been affected as our sense of belonging has expanded from the family, tribe or village to encompass considerably larger areas such as cities and countries. Research has shown that the feel-ing of working for the common good is strongest in groups consisting of up to 150 people. For instance, vil-lages of hunter-gatherers around the world often consist of around 150 people. In the same way, military units usually consist of about 150 people, and should never exceed 200. Beyond this, the feeling of community is diluted, and this is the reason why well-functioning units, whether they be armies, businesses or villages, generally do not consist of a greater number of individuals.

If the total number is greater, then the feeling of community decreases and individualism increases. We need only look at an international football match, however, to realise that this feeling of belonging can encompass considerably more than 150 people. The feeling of belonging we nonetheless experience is enough for us to do our bit towards a well-functioning society.

There may be several reasons why societies often have well-functioning ethics. One possibility is that this is a social construction, that human beings have created ethics in order to have well-functioning societies. Another possibility is that our ethical capacity is innate, that we are born with genes which dispose us towards developing ethical behaviour. And even if the ethical principles and tools used by an individual may be social constructions, this does not mean that there are no genetic preconditions.

What has formed this aspect of human beings, like so much else, is evolution. The theory of evolutionary development originally described by Darwin and Wallace in the mid-nineteenth century has in most respects shown itself to be correct. Species arise from one another through a process which involves mutations in the DNA, which sometimes leads to offspring being born with different characteristics to those of the previous generation. If this difference gives the offspring better chances of surviving and producing its own offspring, then this is an evolutionary advantage, and the mutation is transmitted down through the species' DNA. If the mutation does not give improved characteristics, as is usually the case, or leads to decreased chances of survival and reproduction, then this new characteristic will not be passed on to future generations. In this way new characteristics and species are *selected*, through a process that has been going on for billions of years, from the first simple single-celled organism to the species that inhabit our planet today.

'Survival of the fittest' is a principal theme of the theory of evolution. It means that whoever is best adapted to circumstances (which can vary between different niches in nature) has the best chances of survival. In this respect, competition in nature is ruthless.

The phrase has given rise to the misconception that evolution gives an advantage to those individuals who look after their own selfish interests. But 'survival of the fittest' does not mean, as it is often interpreted, that 'the strongest survives', but that 'the best adapted survives'. This clearly means something entirely different from the idea that an individual should merely club his competitors on the head and then drag his newly claimed sexual partner away to transmit his genes to the next generation. The ability to survive is linked to a series of factors other than mere physical strength and egotism.

One example of characteristics which have been selected because they give rise to improved chances of survival and reproduction are those which enable functioning in a group. Without well-functioning groups and societies, mankind would be ill-equipped in the competition for survival. Human-shaped beings without the capacity for empathetic, altruistic and ethical thought would not survive long, because they would either wipe each other out, or perish because they could not come together to defend themselves against the dangers of the world around them.

If it were the case that ethical thinking and the capacity to be kind turned out to be an advantage for survival in the evolutionary game, this would be an argument for kindness being a winning concept. If the ability to cooperate, altruism and generosity are advantages in the competition between species to be best adapted for survival, this is a strong argument for the fact that we win by being good.

So let us look at the neighbours who share the biosphere of this planet with us, to see if they exhibit qualities which – if they existed in human beings – would be characterised as kindness and ethical thinking. If they have characteristics which are reminiscent of our own ethical functions, this is a strong argument in favour of ethical abilities being innate and built into our genes and physiology. And because nature only selects characteristics that give us an advantage when it comes to survival, this would argue in favour of ethical thinking being a path to success.

So what about animals? Are there any studies which suggest that they have an in-built ability to care for members of the same species? Are there any studies which suggest that they have the capacity to prioritise the welfare

of others over selfishness? It turns out that there are countless examples of animals acting in ways that benefit the
group rather than the individual. One example is birds.

If a bird in a flock catches sight of a bird of prey, it gives
a warning cry at once. This obviously exposes the calling
bird to great danger because it risks drawing the attention
of the bird of prey to itself, but on the other hand the
whole flock gains the chance to escape. If the bird was not
interested in the safety of its fellows, it would naturally
have been better for it to fly off, leaving the bird of prey
to attack the birds in the flock which, unconcerned, had
stayed behind.

In a similar way, crows that find a dead animal will
inform their fellows at once with loud cries, so that they
can also eat. In spite of the fact that this means there will
be less food for the discoverer, the crows choose to act
altruistically.

Giving presents to each other is a widespread social
convention among human beings. Expensive gifts are expressions of generosity, and generally make a good impression
on those around us. Giving presents is, among other things,
a common occurrence in the courtship of a partner.

But human beings are not unique in their material generosity. Many animal species give each other gifts, often in
the form of food. Even more uncomplicated creatures
such as dragonflies give each other gifts, when the male is
courting the female. If the female appreciates and accepts
the gift, it leads to sexual intercourse. Material generosity
can be worthwhile, even for animals.

Babbler birds live in flocks, and show a very particular type of altruistic behaviour – they actually fight for the right to help each other, for instance by sharing food. They are thus not content with just being good, but fight to be the most generous. The evolutionary reason for this behaviour has been much discussed. One possible explanation is that as well as the gain to the whole group from the altruistic behaviour, the generous bird impresses those around it and thereby increases its chances of finding a mate with which to breed. As a result, this very specific genetic inheritance is passed on.

Why should birds prioritise their fellows' well-being above their own? In all probability this is the result of instinctive behaviour inherited by the birds. And this is behaviour which is reminiscent of human beings' ethical and altruistic capacities.

What about animals closer to us in evolutionary development – mammals? Bats are predators that cannot last more than two days without food. It has been shown that vampire bats have 'friends' with whom they share their food if the other has failed to find food for itself. A vampire bat will vomit up the blood it has sucked during the night from an animal to give its 'friend' a good feed. The two bats in a 'friendship pair' help each other to their mutual benefit.

Whales and dolphins have a well-developed capacity to protect and care for other members of the group. If a sperm whale is injured, the other whales surround it in order to protect it. This behaviour can be exploited by hunters, enabling them to shoot several whales in one go. As we have previously seen, 'kindness' without judgement is not always beneficial to the individual.

In the same way, a group of whales or dolphins has been known to stay near a wounded or sick member of the group which has ended up in shallow water, even if this is potentially dangerous for the entire group. It has also been found that dolphins support their wounded fellows and hold them above the water so they do not drown.

Animals, like human beings, have the ability to learn what is permitted and what is forbidden. A rat can learn to take only a few mouthfuls of food if a researcher claps his hands above the animal after a certain number of bites. But when the researcher leaves the room, the rat eats its fill. If the rat were a human being, we would probably say that it was exhibiting ingratiating behaviour. Other species, such as dogs, can learn what is permitted and forbidden and then internalise this knowledge, so that the behaviour becomes part of its 'personality', independent of whether or not anyone is watching.

We are approaching human beings in the developmental tree, and have now reached our closest relations – the apes. In the case of chimpanzees their genes are 99 per cent the same as ours. Apes also display a range of behaviour that is reminiscent of our own when it comes to caring, generosity and ethics. Apes take care of, protect and help old, wounded or handicapped members of the group. They make sure they have food and adapt the group's movements so that even the weakest can keep up.

One of many examples is the way an ape which later turned out to have been suffering from a kidney disorder was looked after by the group. The sick ape was one of the first allowed to have food, and the whole group took to sleeping on the ground to be close to the ape who could no longer climb. After the ape had died, the group continued to sleep next to the dead body for several days.

Although it would improve the others' chances of moving and collecting food if they did not have to drag the weakest members of the collective with them, they often show great care towards the weak. We might well ask in what way it enhances the survival chances of the species if the oldest members of the group are helped to remain within it. One possibility is that old individuals provide an advantage. In times of drought, they might remember the location of waterholes that have not been visited for several years, for example.

Other evidence of social responsibility is that chimpanzees can mediate between members of the group who have fallen out – and the happiness displayed by the group when the two enemies make up. Maintaining cohesion in a group clearly helps the chances of survival, not merely for humans.

An interesting question is whether this is an expression of empathy – in other words, do the apes have the ability to put each other in one another's position? This question is as yet unanswered, even if studies of apes that are developmentally close to humans have shown behaviour that indicates an empathetic capacity. For instance, chimpanzees carefully and thoroughly wash each other's wounds, in a way which suggests they are conscious of how painful it is to have an open wound.

It is also well known that animals that are developmentally close to humans can have feelings which are expressed in ways that resemble guilt and shame. If a dog has done something forbidden, like chewing a shoe, it exhibits behaviour that is almost a caricature of an ashamed human being (from the dog's perspective, our ashamed behaviour is obviously a caricature of their behaviour). Apes who have done something forbidden can behave in a 'guilty' way towards other members of the group, even if it is clear that the others do not know what has happened. The similarity to the human conscience is striking, even if we naturally cannot know what the animals are thinking deep inside.

Animals can behave in ways that remind us of human moral characteristics – for instance, having and observing social rules, showing feelings of guilt, caring for the weak, punishing crimes which break rules, mediating in fights – in other words, feelings and activities that aim to foster good relations.

There are various hypotheses as to why animals, like human beings, act altruistically, generously and ethically (in our interpretation of the word). In what way does it benefit the individual in the struggle for survival in nature? One possible explanation is that generosity suggests that the individual has large resources, which can be attractive in the search for a partner with whom to reproduce. In human beings this could most simply be compared to the actions of the courtship phase (and hopefully also afterwards), with its dinner invitations, flowers and expensive presents.

Another hypothesis is usually called family selection and suggests that the individual acts altruistically if it benefits the survival of his or her own genes. If you save two of your children from danger, but die yourself, then you have still made sure that 50% + 50% = 100% of your genes will survive. You could also afford to save four nephews or nieces, or grandchildren (4 × 25%), eight of your cousins (8 × 12.5%), or a sibling, a grandchild and eight second cousins (50% + 25% + 8 × 3.125%).

In this way, birds have been known to protect others in the group or organise food for them, because some in the group belong to their own family. Insects that live in societies in which practically every individual is related can commit great deeds for the collective. In human beings, perhaps nepotism can be seen as a variant of family selection.

A further hypothesis is called reciprocal altruism. It suggests that individuals are generous and altruistic because they expect the same in return. 'You scratch my back and I'll scratch yours' is a well-known phrase among humans, and it turns out that a lot of animals expect this as well. Studies of chimpanzees, for instance, have shown that they would rather share food with members of a group from whom they have previously received food, and that this generous behaviour is independent of family ties.

It is important to stress that there are also examples of situations where animals behave in a less altruistic or caring way. Animals of the same species may well harass one another, fight each other to the death, and abandon their sick, old and weak. Like us, animals can be evil towards each other. And like us, animals can do great damage to other species, for instance in their search for food. So we ought to remember that human beings, unlike other species, have activists who campaign for animal rights, and that a lot of people feel great sympathy for the plight of animals. Lest anyone suggest that humans are less 'good' than other animals, we should not forget this compassion for other species, which makes us unique in the animal kingdom.

So ought we to call animals' behaviour towards one another ethical? It depends rather upon your definition. Ethics presupposes a certain degree of reflection, and it is unclear whether even our closest relatives, the apes, possess this analytical capacity to any great extent. On the other hand, the apes do exhibit behaviour which is so close to our own in respect of ethics, goodness and compassion that you cannot but be surprised. And it seems unlikely that it should be a question of wildly differing motivations that make an ape and a human being take care of a wounded or sick member of the group. A more plausible explanation is that the capacity for compassion, altruism and goodness is part of our genetic inheritance, which has been selected during the course of evolution. This in turn leads to the conclusion that in the natural struggle for survival, goodness, kindness and well-functioning ethics are beneficial. Caring for our fellows has therefore in all likelihood contributed to the evolutionary success of human beings.

Studies of human beings

One of the preconditions for a group to function well is an ethical framework which regulates interaction between the members of the group. We need a society which is just, loyal, caring when we need help, supportive when we need to develop, and so on. And we human beings are willing to contribute to such a society.

But goodness is not just learned behaviour. There have been studies made of children of approximately one year of age. Family members were asked to demonstrate feelings of sorrow, pain and discomfort for the children. It turned out that these young children already had the ability to imagine someone else's suffering, and had developed the capacity to comfort, by patting and hugging.

One remarkable discovery was that even new-born babies have the basics of an empathetic ability. When new-born infants hear other babies cry, they start to cry as well. This is not because they are disturbed by the noise, because other noises do not affect them in the same way.

Interestingly, young girls had a more pronounced ability to sympathise with the suffering of others than boys. Studies of adults have shown that men and women have the same ability to understand others' feelings, but that women are more affected emotionally.

How much of our goodness and wickedness depends on our genes, and how much on our upbringing and other so-called environmental factors? Research into twins has provided information about what forms these characteristics.

Twins are either derived from one and the same egg, which means that they are genetically identical, or from two eggs, in which case they share half of their genes (as is also the case with normal siblings). It has been shown by studying both types of twins with the help of psychological tests that approximately half of characteristics such as altruism, the ability to nurture and empathy are determined by our genes. The degree of aggression is similarly half-determined by inheritance.

We are evidently born with a fairly well-developed tendency towards goodness, but the surrounding environment can have an effect on how we develop. Since less kind characteristics such as aggression have not been weeded out by evolution, we can also conclude that a certain level of less altruistic characteristics can enhance our chances of survival.

Nature is so ingeniously constructed that it links certain factors that are required for survival to positive experience.

This is why sexual activity feels pleasurable, caring for our offspring feels good, and eating is enjoyable. If we did not experience these as positive, we would not reproduce, take care of our children or feed ourselves. And the consequence would naturally be that we would die out, both as individuals and as a species.

Studies have also shown that cooperation between people gives rise to the same physiological effects in the brain as when we take pleasure-enhancing drugs. Consequently we cooperate and help others partly because it gives us a feeling of pleasure.

This is one example of how human beings, through evolution, have developed characteristics that favour cooperation. If it did not feel good, we would not co-operate with each other like we do. And because the desire to cooperate is a characteristic which enhances the human species' ability to survive and reproduce, nature, through evolution, has made sure that this characteristic is linked to something that feels good. Here, once again, we have an egotistical reason for being good. Good deeds act like drugs, but without the side effects.

How else do we benefit from doing good, besides the fact that it gives us pleasurable sensations? In experiments people in a group were asked to give money to each other. The participants did not know who they received the money from, merely how much the other people had shared of their resources. The tendency was always clear. People were more inclined to share their own money with those who were generous towards others. Those who gave most also received most, not necessarily from those to whom they had given money. We benefit from being generous, particularly towards those who in turn are 'good', whereas those who 'let people down' lose. And if we are generous towards our fellows, it means that they are generous towards others. A ripple effect arises which benefits everyone.

That we become helpful and generous if we ourselves are treated well has been underlined by an experiment conducted on people making calls from a payphone. In half of the cases, a coin had been left in the slot for returned money. Just as the unknowing participants left the phone box – after either receiving a coin or not – a woman went past and dropped a folder of papers on the ground. It turned out that almost nine out of ten of those who had found money in the slot helped her to gather up the paper, whereas only a few of those who had not found any money (4 per cent) helped her.

It has also been shown that students in a library were more inclined to help another student if they had been given a biscuit. Clearly we do not have to receive large material rewards in order to become positively inclined towards those around us.

In another interesting study, free office stationery was distributed to certain households, while others received nothing. Researchers then phoned the households, explained that they had dialled the wrong number, but had no more money left, and asked the person at the end of the line to call a garage which could collect the caller's car. Those who had received free stationery were more inclined to help. And finally, a further study has actually showed something that we could all have guessed: diners in restaurants give more tips on sunny days than when it is cloudy.

But the fact that we are more inclined to help others if we ourselves are well treated does not only apply to gifts. Experiments have been conducted where the participants have taken a test and then – regardless of the actual results – been told that they have done either well or badly. Then the participants were tested in two ways. The first variant involved the researcher leaving the room, where there was also a charity collection box. It turned out that those who had been told that they had done well were more likely to donate money. In the second variant, the researcher returned with a pile of books which he then dropped on the floor. Those who had been told they had done well were more likely to help pick the books up.

This experiment shows that we treat those around us well if we ourselves are treated well. It does not seem to make any difference whether we are treated well by a fellow human being or a piece of machinery. The result is that the better we behave towards our fellows, the better our fellows behave towards us. And, best of all, they are not only good towards us. They also behave more kindly towards other people. And these people in turn behave more kindly towards others, and so on. In this way our good deeds spread out like ripples on a pond. We are not powerless. We can do a great deal for those around us, and thus for ourselves. In the end it is probably true – a single person really can influence the whole world.

Another interesting observation is that generosity leads us to perform better. Small gifts in the form of coins or sweets lead to improvements in memory, ability to learn, creativity and problem-solving. It has been shown that doctors who are given small gifts – sweets, for instance – and then perform a diagnosis on an imaginary patient do so faster and better than doctors who have not received a gift. Those doctors who received a gift were also less likely to draw quick conclusions. Clearly, generosity not only means that we become more helpful, but also that we can do things better.

But human beings have also been blessed with a strong sense of justice. We are even willing to sacrifice our own assets to remedy what we perceive to be unjust behaviour in others. This was shown by an experiment known as the Ultimatum Game, where the participants were given a sum of money – approximately £100 – and urged to share the money with a fellow player. The problem was that participants could only suggest a sum of money once, and if this was rejected then neither of them would get any money. So the players had to be generous enough that the other player could accept their offer.

More than two thirds of participants chose to offer amounts equal to 40–50 per cent of the total, and these offers were usually accepted. But some participants chose to offer less. It turned out that people tend to accept amounts down to about 30 per cent of the total sum. Most offers below this amount were rejected, so no one received any money.

People clearly have an innate feeling for what is right, and are willing to go without money in order to assert this need for justice. That this is a matter of not accepting unjust solutions is underlined by the fact that the same experiment was conducted with a computer sharing out the money. It turned out that people were prepared to accept extremely low offers from a computer.

The importance of punishment on our behaviour has been discussed. For instance, does crime in society decrease if we punish criminals? There are studies which show that not only rewards, but also punishment can have a positive impact on the way people cooperate. One example is the Public Goods Game.

In this experiment each participant is given a sum of money equivalent to about £10. They have the chance either to keep the money or, without knowing how the other three players will act, to put the money in a collective pot, where the money is first doubled, then shared equally between the players. If all the players put all their money in the pot, they would therefore each get £20 back. But if only one person put their money in the pot, they would only get £5 back – and lose £5 – while the other players would end up with £15.

The result showed that players were, on average, prepared to put 40–60 per cent of their money into the pot.

But if the game is played several times in succession, the players become progressively less inclined to put money in the pot – presumably because they realise that not everyone is contributing. The interesting thing is that if players have the chance to punish each other for meanness by forcing the players to pay a certain amount, then more and more players begin to put all their money in the pot. Players are willing to punish other players' meanness, even if it means that they themselves have to pay every time they impose a punishment. With a system of punishments in place, eventually three-quarters of the players put all of their money into the pot. Altering the rules of the game to make it obvious that you lose by being selfish therefore leads to a situation where everyone benefits.

The results of these experiments are self-evident. That we have a desire to cooperate and do good for each other is not just something we can conclude through our contacts with our fellows – scientific studies show that these qualities exist within us. We are ethical beings who like to be generous, particularly if others are good towards us. We appreciate justice and we react against injustice, even at our own expense. We clearly have a lot of good in us, and, best of all, goodness pays off. People become good towards those who are good towards them, but at the same time they also become good towards others. One kind deed can thus have a domino effect.

The religious view

In large-scale opinion polls in Sweden, almost 60 per cent of those asked said that they believed in the existence of God. A little more than 10 per cent said that they did not believe in God; the remainder were unsure, to a greater or lesser degree. Clearly there are many people who either believe or who have an open mind about whether religions may be correct, at least in some of their beliefs. Because religions often claim ethics to be important, and that good deeds get their reward while evil is punished, I shall also look at the religious arguments for the suggestion that we benefit from doing good. Then it is up to each of us whether to believe that religious suppositions have a basis in reality.

It is estimated that there are approximately 3,000 religions on the planet. Many of these have few followers, while others are global religions with millions of followers. In a comparison of religions, it is soon discovered that they vary in certain ways. They differ, for instance, in traditions, rites, in their beliefs in a deity or deities, their view of the meaning of life, and descriptions of what happens to us beyond death.

At the same time, there are aspects of religions which are strikingly similar, even if the different religions have sprung up in widely differing times and cultures.

One example of this is ethics. Practically all religions have ethics at their absolute core, and offer us guidance, rules and laws for how we should live our lives. According to these religions, one of our main tasks is to choose good and reject evil deeds.

The first five books of the Bible, the Pentateuch, are full of laws and rules governing how people should behave. For the Jewish, ethics can be added from other books in the Old Testament, the Talmud, which contains interpretations of the Bible's laws, as well as a series of other scriptures. There was a revolution within Judaism after the destruction of the Second Temple in the year AD70, when literal interpretation of certain hair-raising laws and punishments was abandoned.

For Christianity, we must add the New Testament, which for instance raises ethical norms above strict adherence to the law. One recurrent theme in Christianity is love of one's neighbour, meaning that we should not only do good for our fellows, but also strive to love them.

The most important book in Islam is the Koran, which is a compilation of the revelations of the Prophet Mohammed. Islamic law, the Sharia, is also based upon the Sunna, which is the application of the teachings of the Prophet Mohammed, as well as other scriptures.

One eastern religion in which ethics is highlighted is Confucianism, which stresses ethics and etiquette above other aspects of religion. Confucius proposed that man is good by nature, but that a lack of knowledge could lead to evil. The main source for Confucianism in respect of ethical behaviour are the written conversations of Confucius.

Both Hinduism and Buddhism have books governing ethics and law. Within Hinduism there are the law books, the Dharmasastra, for instance. And Buddhism has the Vinaya Pitaka, which describes how monks and nuns should live. Both of these religions stress as a central theme the importance of how we treat our fellow human beings.

Taoism does not attach such significance to specific laws and rules, but proposes that for a complete person good deeds will come by themselves. People should strive for wisdom: 'The man who has wisdom does not sin, he ceases to do evil and through his wisdom annuls the evils of his former life.'

An example of the conformity between different religions is that the Golden Rule is a basic ethical principle. All the global religions have their variant of the Golden Rule. Here are a few examples:

- What is hateful to you, do not do to your neighbour. (Judaism) [Talmud, Shabbat 3id]
- All things whatsoever ye would that men should do to you, do ye even so to them. (Christianity) [Matthew 7:12]
- No one of you is a believer until he desires for his brother that which he desires for himself. (Islam) [Sunnah]
- Do not do to others what you would not like yourself. (Confucianism) [Analects 12:2]
- Regard your neighbour's gain as your gain, and your neighbour's loss as your own loss. (Taoism) [Tai Shang Kan Yin P'ien]

- Hurt not others in ways that you yourself would find hurtful. (Buddhism) [Udana-Varga 5:1]
- Seeing oneself in all and all in oneself, one does not injure others because that means injury to oneself. [from Nikhilananda Essence of Hinduism quoting Bhagavadgita]

Many religions, arising from different sources, combine in the same ethical principle: the way in which we ourselves wish to be treated should be our guide as to how we treat others.

Nor is this the only common theme between religions regarding ethics. Most religions teach that there is a system of rewards and punishments associated with how we treat our fellows and the world around us. This means that good deeds have a positive effect which exceeds that of the deed itself. In the same way, an evil deed has negative consequences which exceed those of the direct results of the deed itself. Good deeds have their reward, either in this life or the next. Evil deeds have their punishment, either in this life or the next. Many religions claim that there is a 'natural law' which regulates the consequences of our actions.

Judaism is a religion bound by laws, in other words a religion which stresses the importance of following laws and rules. At the same time, the importance of being good in a broader perspective is underlined. In the Talmud it says: 'Loving kindness is greater than laws; and the charities of life are more than all ceremonies.' After the

Second Temple had been destroyed in AD70, the question arose as to why this calamity had happened. One response was that it did not depend upon mankind having sinned, but upon mankind having followed the law too strictly. This emphasises the fact that rules should function as guides, but that they do not absolve humankind from the responsibility to do good. Individual goodness is valued higher than strict adherence to the law, rites and traditions.

According to Judaism, we should live an ethical life because this is our task, but also because it will benefit us. Even if Jewish scriptures express surprise at the fact that the system is not entirely fair − which is apparent, for instance, in Ecclesiastes: 'All things have I seen in the days of my vanity: there is a just man that perisheth in his righteousness, and there is a wicked man that prolongeth his life in his wickedness' [7:15] − the Jewish perception is that good deeds will receive their reward, and evil deeds their punishment. In Deuteronomy it says: 'And thou shalt do that which is right and good in the sight of the Lord: that it may be well with thee' [6:18], and in the Book of Job it says the following about God's view of mankind's actions: 'He repays a man for what he has done; he brings upon him what his conduct deserves.' [34:11] The reward and punishment may come either in this life or after death. A person who has lived a wicked life may miss out on life after death, while someone who has been good will be granted a life after this one. Exactly what form this life after death will take has never been agreed upon within Judaism, but it is assumed that God will somehow arrange this.

It is thus a question of a choice of paths in life. If we start to sin, we are likely to continue to sin, whereas if we do good deeds, so-called mitzvot, we will have a tendency to continue doing so. Human beings can differentiate between good and evil, and it is our task to control our evil impulses and strive to do good. We will thereby become 'righteous' and – as it says in the Talmud – 'Greater are the righteous than the ministering angels'.

According to Judaism, human beings have the chance to establish 'The Kingdom of God', in other words a paradisical existence here on earth. What is required, among other things, for this to happen, is that a sufficient number of people live an ethical life in goodness, and caring for their fellows. So we not only do good deeds for the sake of others and ourselves, but for the whole world.

In Christianity there is a strong connection between right faith and salvation. A precondition for human beings to be granted eternal life is faith in Jesus as the Messiah (Christos in Greek). According to John's Gospel, Jesus said: 'I am the resurrection and the life: he that believeth in me, though he were dead, yet shall he live.' [11:25]

According to the Christian creed, various things can happen when we die. We can end up in heaven, a life in the presence of God, but we can also end up in purgatory (which has, however, been abolished within Protestantism), or in hell. Even if our destination is determined by our faith, our deeds can still be significant. One example of this attitude occurs in the Epistle of James: 'But wilt thou know, O vain man, that faith without works is dead?' [2:20]

Today the representatives of Christianity are sometimes unwilling to speak of purgatory and hell, and often suggest that these represent various emotional states we can attain when we die, where our regret at the evil we have done can cause us torment.

According to Christianity the good, led by God, are fighting against the evil, sometimes defined as being led by the devil. As human beings, we have to adopt a stance for either good or evil, and Christianity encourages us to choose the good. In this way we can all contribute towards a better world.

Jesus is the example that human beings should try to emulate in goodness, forgiveness and love, and if people live in his image they can contribute to a better world. So we should do good deeds for their own sake, and without thinking of the rewards, but it will nonetheless have positive consequences if human beings do good. In the words of the preacher and author William Penn: 'He that does good for good's sake seeks neither paradise nor reward, but he is sure of both in the end.'

According to Christianity, the right attitude is an important aspect of life. The Christian monk and mystic Master Eckehart expressed this in the following words: 'If you are righteous, that what you do will also be righteous.'

Christianity also struggles with the problem of the innocent being afflicted by suffering, and asks the question of how God can accept that someone who has done nothing wrong should suffer. A classic example is the dialogue between Ivan and Alyosha in Dostoevsky's *The Brothers Karamazov*. Ivan tells his brother how a five-year-old child was repeatedly beaten by its parents, and in vain prays to God for help: 'Not even a whole world of knowledge is worth the price of such a small child's tears.'

According to Islam, God created humankind with a special nature – fitrah – in order that we might worship God. An important way of doing this is by treating our fellows well. But human beings have also been blessed with an ego – nafs – which drags us down and encourages us to do evil. Evil deeds make the ego strong and the heart weak, whereas good deeds make the ego weak and the heart strong. We must strive to stop the ego taking charge, and work for the victory of the forces of good.

People should do good deeds, such as helping the poor and the suffering and being generous, and refrain from doing evil. The Koran stresses that it is not enough to be afraid of God and to pray regularly, but that it is also a question of everyday ethics: 'So woe to the worshippers Who are neglectful of their prayers, Those who (want but) to be seen (of men), But refuse (to supply) (even) neighbourly needs.'

So what are the advantages of doing good? An important reason for living an ethical life is that it is in our innermost nature to do good. If we do not choose to exist in this way, we are living a false life, we are breaking against our own nature. If we are good, on the other hand, we have a good inner life, we live in the light. In the Koran it says: 'Whoever rejects evil and believes in Allah hath grasped the most trustworthy hand-hold, that never breaks. And Allah heareth and knoweth all things.'

A further aspect is life after death. According to Islam, the soul exists before a person is born, and is united with its predetermined body at birth. On death, the soul is separated from the body only to be reunited with it at the resurrection on the Day of Judgement. On this day, every human being shall answer for his or her deeds. They will then receive their book, in which the angels have inscribed the good and evil deeds they have committed during their life. These deeds are weighed on scales. Those who have been faithful and done good deeds will enter paradise, while those who have not had the correct faith and have been evil will enter hell. Because God is merciful, many of those who enter hell will reach paradise in time. But not all, for instance those who have lacked all trace of belief in God.

In this way Islam stresses the fact that our deeds will have eternal consequences, and that a good life gives a person an advantage, both in this life and the next. In the words of the Koran: 'If anyone does a righteous deed, it ensures to the benefit of his own soul; if he does evil, it works against (his own soul).'

★

According to the monotheistic religions, we live one life, die, and then have an existence after death which is partly determined by our deeds in life. Eastern religions like Hinduism and Buddhism differ from monotheistic faiths by proclaiming that we do not live just one life, but many lives. We are born, live one life and die, and are then born again to a new life, a new death, a new birth, and so on. We may be reborn as a human being, but also as an animal. Life, according to this belief in reincarnation, is thus circular.

What is it that determines what sort of existence awaits us after each new birth? It is karma, which is our collected deeds throughout the previous life. The more good deeds we have done, the better the existence that awaits us in our new life. But if we have done bad deeds and not enough good, we will be reborn as a lower being, possibly even as an animal. Good deeds are therefore rewarded even according to these religions, while bad deeds are punished.

According to Hinduism, human beings have a soul which is reborn in the new body. The karma we have collected during our life determines where the soul ends up in the new life. It is therefore important that each person strives to do good, in order to ensure a good rebirth. There is an eternal law, dharma, which gives good and evil deeds their just reward. Like the monotheistic religions, Hinduism foresees an end to our era. Then the god Vishnu will manifest himself and punish those who have done evil and inaugurate a new and happy era.

According to Buddhism, there is a moral world-order based upon the laws of cause and effect. We cannot evade the consequences of our bad deeds – if they do not come in this life, they will come in the next. Buddhism does not speak of a soul, but our karma follows us from our previous lives, so the consequences of our deeds follow us into our rebirth. Human beings should strive to do good deeds and refrain from doing evil, not least because things will then go well for us. In the words of Buddha: 'Neither fire nor wind, neither birth nor death, can erase our good deeds.'

The only way in which we can break this eternal cycle is by collecting only good karma. Then we can enter a higher, indescribable existence, known within Hinduism as moksha, and within Buddhism as nirvana.

Also Confucianism suggests that it is to our advantage to do good for others. Confucius refrained from speculation about a life after this one, but nonetheless claimed adamantly that good deeds have positive consequences: 'He who cares for others' progress has already secured his own.'

According to Taoism, an ethical stance is the natural way of living. To live in a righteous way is to live in harmony with nature. Evil deeds depend on a lack of knowledge, and clash with the harmony of the world. This has negative consequences, both for the individual and for society: 'Their recompenses follow good and evil as the shadow follows the substance.'

★

It is difficult to write about religious ethics without asking whether religions are always good examples from an ethical point of view. The answer, of course, is no. Religion has been used throughout the ages by unscrupulous people to commit unethical deeds. If we read the Old Testament, we see that this was the case even thousands of years ago, and people today commit atrocious acts in the name of religion. Religious fundamentalism is today one of the great dangers facing the world.

Religions have a dark side, but this does not mean that they lack a lighter side. In many respects, religions have been the bearers of the ethical thinking that societies need in order to function. This does not mean that religions are a precondition for ethical thought, but that religions have done, and still do, a great deal to maintain ethical structures. We do not always remember that the ethics of the Western world, whose norms we usually regard as self-evident, are largely based upon the Judeo-Christian tradition.

Many religions agree that ethics is a central aspect of our lives, and that good deeds receive their reward, while bad deeds are punished, either in this life or after death. Regardless of the religion, this is advanced as an argument for why we should be good towards our fellow human beings and the world around us.

Does any of this actually matter? Do we really need to worry about what 'a few old religions' have to say about the importance of being good? Has ethics been linked to religion in order to keep us under control, so that our societies are decent, as some people have suggested? Or should we believe that there is a divine natural law that means that we benefit from being good and lose out if we let our bad side prevail?

I do not have the answer to this question. I am myself agnostic, which means both that I think there is no certain evidence for the existence of divine power or global order, but also that I think there is no evidence for the opposite. But I do believe that the hypothesis that religions advance – of a natural law which leads to our deeds having consequences for us – is possible and worth taking seriously. And I am evidently not alone in this belief. In an opinion poll in Sweden, 60 per cent of those asked said that they believed that sooner or later we will be held responsible for our actions.

So I do not think we can disregard the arguments proposed by religions about why we should do good and avoid evil. Perhaps they are wrong. But on the other hand, imagine that they are right – that would not be much fun for anyone who has not been kind. Eternity is rather longer than the nearly eighty years the average western European lives. Perhaps we are prepared to take the risk, perhaps not. Regardless of this, though, the religious view of the question of good and evil is merely another reason for doing good, and definitely not an argument for the reverse.

Other observations

As we have already seen, scientific studies indicate that we have an inherited ethical capacity which gives us greater chances of survival, and that we gain from being kind and good. On top of this there is the religious teaching that we benefit from being ethical. But there are also anecdotal observations and logical conclusions which show that we win by being kind. I have put these arguments together in this section.

According to one point of view, kindness means always thinking of others and never about yourself, and that you should even put others' welfare above your own. Such people do exist, but they are unusual. The majority of kind people (and deeds) are driven by various egotistical motivations.

What sort of selfish reasons are there for doing good deeds and avoiding wicked ones? Here are a few suggestions.

- Getting appreciation in return.
- Avoiding conflict.
- Feeling that you are a good person (people who are driven by this motivation often have an inner perception of themselves as evil, which has generally been instilled in them in early childhood).
- Becoming popular.
- Cooperating well with other people.

- Avoiding having a guilty conscience.
- Getting praise.
- Avoiding the negative opinion of those around us.
- Gaining friends.
- Avoiding punishment for breaking the law.
- Not having to stand seeing other people suffer.
- Feeling needed.
- Caring for our offspring, who in some ways are parts of ourselves.
- Avoiding 'our sins coming back to haunt us'.
- Having a good relationship with a higher power.
- Getting a better life after death.

These motivations can be divided into four groups:
- those which stem from our self-image;
- those which affect our relations with people close to us;
- those which affect our relations with society;
- those which affect our relations with a higher power.

We are social creatures, and therefore have a need to function in a context where our image – in both our own eyes and those of the world around us – is a positive one. Why do firemen save lives at the risk of their own? Why do nurses look after their patients with such care? Why do idealists write articles in an attempt to influence the world for the better? Why do people take care of friends who are sad? Why do politicians want to carry out welfare reforms?

Perhaps they are driven by a desire to realise their ideas?

Perhaps they want to earn a living? Perhaps they are curious? Perhaps they crave attention? Perhaps they want to feel needed? Perhaps they long for power? The reason is actually quite unimportant, as long as it benefits all of us.

Sometimes we carry out deeds which are entirely devoid of egotistical motives, and are purely aimed at the needs of others – that much is true. But I simply cannot see that these deeds are 'better' than those which have an element of selfish calculation. In my eyes, the fact that kind deeds are often egotistical does not detract from the beauty that I see in the encounter with goodness and compassion.

'So,' some people would say, 'what sort of goodness is it that comes from being selfish? That's not goodness, it's egotism!' This argument is based upon a common mis-conception, that egotism and goodness are opposites. This is not the case. We have every right in the world to be good for selfish reasons.

The Dalai Lama has wisely said this about egotistical people: 'Foolish selfish people are always thinking of themselves, and the result is negative. Wise selfish people think of others, help others as much as they can, and the result is that they too receive benefits.'

The Dalai Lama means that we can perfectly well be kind from egotistical motives. We need not be righteous for anyone else's sake but our own. It is entirely human to be good for egotistical reasons. And he also supports the central message of this chapter, that we gain from being good. Goodness and kindness are rewarded, whereas those inclined otherwise will be losers.

With these words, the Dalai Lama underlines the fact that the motivation behind the deed is not the important thing, but rather the deed itself. As we have already discussed: it is *not* the thought that counts, but the deed – what we do.

If much of the good that we do occurs for egotistical reasons, then this conclusion follows logically: good deeds, compassion for our fellows, kindness, really do benefit us. Otherwise good deeds would lead to the opposite, that we lose out, and that is not compatible with the idea that we do good for our own sake. That human beings, with all their empirical accumulated experience, should be so thoroughly stupid as to do a load of good only to lose out as a result – I have a lot of trouble trying to imagine that.

If things should happen to be so ingeniously constructed – that we benefit if we do good deeds and are kind – is there any reason why we should not take advantage of this simple fact, that good deeds get their reward?

How does this work on a societal level? Is there evidence to show that 'good' cultures with freedom of expression, legal protection, personal autonomy and democratic rights manage better than other cultures?

Freedom House is a US-based politically independent organisation which each year evaluates every country and grades them according to their political rights and civil liberties. Then countries are divided into free, partially free, and not free. At the end of 2005, eighty-nine countries were deemed to be free (46 per cent), fifty-six countries were partially free (30 per cent), and forty-five countries were not free (24 per cent). Of the world's population, 46 per cent lived in free countries, 18 per cent in partially free countries, and 36 per cent in not free countries.

The conclusions that Freedom House comes to have been used in studies in which this information is compared with economic and social data. The results show that out of low-income countries with an annual gross national income (GNI) lower than $1,500 per person, 16 per cent were free countries, while the remaining 84 per cent were partially free or not free countries. High-income countries (annual GNI higher than $6,000 per person) were 80 per cent free countries, while the remaining 20 per cent were either partially free or not free. Other studies indicate that the democracies with liberties and legal protection are the countries whose populations do best in terms of economic development, lifespan, equality and literacy.

There are other differences which become apparent in a comparison between democracies and dictatorships. For instance, sixty catastrophic famines during the twentieth century, which led to the deaths of at least 86 million people, were studied. Of these famines, *none* occurred in a country with democracy and freedom.

A further interesting observation is based upon studies of international wars between 1816 and 1991, conducted by Jack Levy. During these 175 years there were approximately seventy wars, of which several involved considerably more than two countries. According to the common definitions of democracy and of war, during these 175 years there was not a single instance of two democracies being involved in a regular war with each other. Two borderline cases were when Great Britain declared war on Finland during the Second World War, without this leading to hostilities between the two countries, and warlike skirmishes with few casualties between Peru and Ecuador from 1981 onwards.

Finally, there have been studies of state-sponsored murder of civilians. There is no definitive data identifying how many innocent people have been killed in this way during the twentieth century, but it may be a little short of 200 million people. Estimates indicate that non-democratic countries accounted for between 98 and 99 per cent of these murders. The approximately two million civilians killed by the actions of democratic countries include, for instance, the victims of the bombing of Dresden and the atomic bombs in Hiroshima and Nagasaki during the Second World War.

The conclusions are evident: forms of government which promote the rule of law, liberty and democracy – concepts which are intimately connected to a comprehensive system of ethics – commonly create better living conditions for their citizens than dictatorships and totalitarian states which lack a fundamentally ethical view of the value of human life.

Unethical regimes have also proved themselves to have poor chances of survival in the modern age. Data from Freedom House covering the past thirty years is unambiguous. The number of not-free countries in 1975 was 41 per cent of the total, but had decreased to 24 per cent in 2005, whereas the number of free countries increased during the same period from 25 per cent to 46 per cent (the number of partially free countries was relatively unchanged: 34 per cent and 30 per cent respectively). More and more dictatorships have been toppled or forced to transfer power to democratic governments, which has led to liberty and civil rights.

There are shortcomings in the democratic system of government. The right decisions are not always taken, and can be the result of ideology which has not been carefully considered or ingratiating behaviour towards a particular group of voters. Those who are best suited to lead may lack the preconditions necessary to succeed in an election. Winston Churchill said in a speech in 1947: 'No one pretends that democracy is perfect or all-wise. Indeed, it has been said that democracy is the worst form of government except all those other forms that have been tried from time to time.' With all its shortcomings, democracy is evidently the best system of government we have managed to create so far. And perhaps the single most important function of democracy is that it stands in the way of other forms of government, such as dictatorship and fascism.

★

What happens in prosperous cultures which are unethical insofar as they do not sufficiently share their wealth with others? An example of inequality between different cultures is the distribution of the world's resources between high-income, middle-income and low-income countries. Almost one billion people live in high-income countries where the GNI per inhabitant is greater than $9,000 per year (according to the World Bank's statistics). In the wealthiest of these countries, the GNI is about $25–30,000 per person per year. Approximately 2.7 billion people live in middle-income countries where the GNI per person is between $735 and $9,000 each year. This means that about 2.5 billion people live in low-income countries with a GNI of less than $735 per person per year.

Another example is that the relationship between the gross national product of the richest countries containing 10 per cent of the world's population and the poorest countries containing 10 per cent of the world's population is more than 140:1, and the tendency during recent decades has been for the difference between rich and poor to increase still further.

The consequences for the poorest countries are evident, for instance in the form of starvation, sickness, a low level of education, and illiteracy. The question is, what are the consequences of this unfair distribution of resources for the rich countries? We still have the most severe consequences ahead of us, but they will come. For instance, the rapid spread of HIV in poor countries will lead to increasing rates of infection in rich countries. Another health problem is the spread of strains of tuberculosis that are immune to most antibiotics.

Environmental damage, which is accelerating in many poor countries, will not only affect these countries, but the whole world. The willingness to take responsibility for the environment is, however, variable also between rich countries.

Unfair distribution between the countries of the world, not only of resources but also of education and liberties, has led to a widespread hatred of wealthy countries. This has had serious consequences in the form of terrorist attacks which have killed many people, and also resulted in large amounts of resources being tied up in the fight against terrorism. And what will happen in the future, if the terrorists get access to weapons of mass destruction, which may only be a matter of time?

These are just a few examples of how a lack of ethical thinking and generosity can end up having negative consequences for all. Globalisation has today led to a situation in which we are in many respects living in a single collective. We have to realise that our responsibility for our neighbour cannot be limited by either national boundaries, religion or ethnic origin. We all bear responsibility for the whole. Human beings have two sides – often generous and altruistic, but sometimes mean and self-interested. For the sake of the planet, let us hope that the good side wins on the global scale. A world in which we share what we have with others is in my view a precondition for our chances of surviving as a species.

★

Finally – with the development of modern computer technology we have new opportunities of studying whether ethical behaviour benefits us. One example is a competition to see which computer program could best play the Prisoners' Dilemma. The Prisoners' Dilemma is an imaginary scenario in which two men who have committed a robbery are arrested in a stolen car by police. But there is no conclusive evidence that they committed the robbery. The police separate them and give each of them a choice. They can either admit their crime and get five years in prison, or deny it and only get one year for car theft. But if one keeps quiet and is betrayed by the other, he will get ten years in prison, while the other will get five years. The problem (for the prisoners, rather than society) is whether or not they can rely on each other. If they can, then they will each get away with just one year in prison. The Prisoners' Dilemma is often played several times, with the result that people gradually change their behaviour when they realise how their opponent is playing.

This game has been used many times to study people's behaviour. When different computer programs competed with each other in playing the Prisoners' Dilemma, it turned out that a very simple program, called Tit-for-Tat, always won. The program was constructed so that it always cooperated (in other words, it always refused to admit to committing the crime) until it met a computer program that betrayed it. In the next round against this program, Tit-for-tat betrayed it (in other words, admitted the crime), only to 'forgive' in the next round and once again try to cooperate. Working for cooperation, but simultaneously being prepared to punish betrayal and thereafter quickly forgive, turned out to be the most successful strategy.

There was also an 'evolutionary' study in which the program that won was permitted to make copies of itself, in an attempt to replicate evolution's 'survival of the fittest'. Tit-for-Tat reproduced and eventually dominated the whole population. This 'ecological experiment' showed once again that behaviour that includes doing good for others and expecting the same in return while not being gullible, leads to a survival advantage.

There is more anecdotal evidence to support what most of us already intuitively sense – that we benefit from doing good, as individuals, as groups and as societies. We only need to look around us to realise this obvious fact – that the world is oppressed by evil, and elevated by goodness.

Conclusion

There are clearly a number of arguments suggesting that human beings should do good and avoid evil. Arguments from evolution, behavioural science, religion and experience are united in the conclusion that we have a lot to gain by being kind. And nothing to gain by being evil. The advantages stretch from increased chances of finding a partner and reproducing our genes, to a happier and more meaningful life, and possibly to a life after death.

The author Ralph Waldo Emerson summed this up: 'It is one of the beautiful compensations of life that no man can sincerely try to help another without helping himself.' Besides the internal sense of satisfaction we get from being kind towards our fellows, good deeds receive their reward, one way or another. Kind people benefit both themselves and others. For this they deserve all our respect and all our admiration.

All of these advantages which come from doing good are different aspects of the concept of 'success'. Everyone wants to be successful in their lives – on this we can all agree. It is just that everyone has different ideas of what the word means. Before we go on to discuss in detail how we can use kindness to become successful, I would therefore like to spend a bit of time discussing what the concept of 'success' might mean.

SUCCESS

There is a wise Chinese tale about success: a poor man lived with his son and their most precious possession – a horse. One day the horse disappeared. When the villagers came to commiserate, the man asked how they knew that what had happened was a setback. After a while the horse came back with a herd of wild horses. The man had suddenly become rich. Again the villagers came, this time to congratulate the man on his great success. Once again he replied with a question: 'How do you know that this is a success?' When the son started breaking in one of the horses, he was thrown off and broke his leg. The leg healed badly, and the son was left with a limp. The villagers came to express their regret at what had befallen the family, and the man replied by wondering how they knew that what had happened was a setback. When war broke out in the country and all the young men were sent to the front, the limping son was let off from serving in the army and could remain at home in safety.

'Success' is an important concept, not least considering that striving for success in various areas of our lives is a potent force for many people. For better or worse, we value our own lives and others on a scale of success.

The concept of success raises a lot of questions: what is it that drives us to perform? How do we try to achieve success? How is success measured? How can it be that what one person regards as success is not seen the same way by someone else? How should we behave in order to feel in our hearts that we are successful?

Basically, words function as conventions which facilitate communication between individuals. This means that everyone who uses a particular language is pretty much agreed on what they are talking about when a specific word is used. Examples of words which comprise strong conventions are 'chair', 'dog', 'person', 'walk', 'smile', 'nose', and so on. There are also conventional words which are more relative. What do I mean, for instance, when I use the word 'love'? Do I mean the same thing as my cousin? Another such word is 'God'. Here there are countless variants of what people mean when they use the word. A third example of a relative conventional word is 'success'. Two people do not usually mean exactly the same thing when they use the word. So it is important to analyse what this word means to us, and how we should interpret our lives in relation to this concept.

The importance of perspective

In the Chinese tale we see how what first looks like success can become the opposite, and vice versa. An ideology, an occurrence, an event can first look like a failure, only to show itself to be a success later. Or the reverse. There are plenty of examples of occurrences, achievements and events which have been re-evaluated with the passage of time.

John Kennedy Toole spent several years trying to get his book, *A Confederacy of Dunces*, published. When he failed to do so, he committed suicide at the age of thirty-two. His mother continued to try to get the book published, and finally succeeded. When the book was published, eleven years after the author's death, it was a great success. It won the most prestigious literary award in the USA, the Pulitzer, and has been translated into eighteen languages. Long after his death, John Kennedy Toole achieved major success, and is today regarded as a great literary talent. Who could have imagined that his book, which first seemed to be a literary failure, would be such a success? Possibly John Kennedy Toole's mother.

In a similar way, what first appears to be a success can become a failure. In the year 279BC, King Pyrrhus won a military victory over the Roman army at Asculum. After losing almost his entire army in the battle, he uttered the famous line: 'One more such victory and we are lost.' Pyrrhus was forced to give up, and abandoned the Italian mainland.

There are many examples of wars which initially seem to be successful for one party, but which later turn and end up with the initial victors not only losing their conquests but also everything they had before they embarked on war. Napoleon and Hitler are two well-known examples of presumptive conquerors of the world who had to watch their initial victories turn to failure.

Even political ideologies have had to face the same fate. With the Russian Revolution in 1917, the communist ideology achieved its first great success. This was followed by many more, and in the early 1980s there were twenty-two communist countries in the world, including the whole of eastern Europe. An impressive and successful ideology, one might think – until it all began to collapse like a house of cards in 1989. Now there are only five countries that call themselves communist (China, Cuba, Laos, North Korea and Vietnam).

Within the world of science, it can take many years before a new hypothesis is universally accepted, which is why so many Nobel Prize winners are grey-haired and walk with a cane.

Ignaz Semmelweis was a Hungarian doctor who worked in Vienna in the mid-nineteenth century. At the time a lot of newly delivered mothers died of puerperal (or childbed) fever. Semmelweis noticed that mortality was considerably higher among women who were looked after by doctors rather than by midwives. When a doctor who had had a cut on his hand when he conducted a post-mortem examination became ill and died of symptoms similar to puerperal fever, Semmelweis drew the conclusion that the cause of puerperal fever was that doctors picked up a dangerous substance from bodies on which they had performed post-mortems and carried it to the women (it later turned out to be bacteria). He introduced a rule that doctors must wash with a chlorine solution before attending a birth.

Semmelweis's thesis was met with strong resistance, and he was actively opposed by the establishment. He became mentally ill and died in a mental institution in 1865, ironically of a bacterial infection caused by a wound on his finger. Semmelweis never experienced the recognition that his work received some years after his death, and today his contribution is regarded as one of the greatest within medical science. Semmelweis is an example of posthumous success.

Sometimes our experience of success is unclear even from a temporal perspective. Zoroastrianism is a religion with two gods, one evil and one good. Life is seen as a struggle between the forces of good and evil, in which good will eventually triumph. Zoroastrianism was the dominant religion in Iran for approximately 1,500 years, and also spread to other parts of the world. During the seventh century Islam began to spread, and Zoroastrianism became increasingly superseded. Today there are only about 200,000 practitioners of the religion in the whole world. But the influence of Zoroastrianism can be seen in Judaism, Christianity, Islam and Buddhism. Success or not?

We cannot state with any confidence which events and people of today will be regarded as successful in the future. Richard Nixon's presidency, once he had become the only American president so far to have been forced to resign, was regarded as a failure, but it has been re-evaluated, partly because of his efforts to improve relations with China and the then Soviet Union.

We have had sports stars whom we have praised for their fantastic achievements. And then there comes the day when it turns out that they were using prohibited drugs. Suddenly their success is transformed into deepest humiliation. Perhaps the time will come – with access to increasingly sensitive tests – when even more of today's sports stars will turn out to have been drugged.

In order to confirm that an event or an achievement has been successful, we need a long perspective, and even with this perspective success can be difficult to analyse. But this is not the only problem with evaluating success.

The dream of success

We all have an idea of what success means. We fantasise about what it would be like if we were to achieve the goals we most cherish. These goals vary between individuals, but also between different societies and eras. In certain cultures people's success was judged according to how strong they were. Of course, this mainly concerned men. Women, in turn, were judged by how many children they gave birth to, or by the status of the man they married, which is scarcely something which resonates well in today's view of society. In other societies success was evaluated according to how wise people were. And in certain cultures it was – and is – wealth that denotes success.

One common criterion of success today is fame. One's celebrity may be the result of many different things – acting, writing, participating in docusoaps, politics, business leadership and so on. Of course there are also people who become famous for negative reasons, through crime or various forms of scandal. In such cases it is more a case of being infamous than famous.

So are we always content when we achieve the goals we have set ourselves? Sadly not. We are often fooled into thinking that if only we could achieve these goals, we would be happy and content. If only we had more money, or a nicer house, or more responsibility at work, or the perfect partner, then we would be happy with life.

Studies in the USA have shown that over 70 per cent of college students thought that wealth was an important goal in life (while only about 40 per cent thought that the development of a meaningful philosophy of life was important). But what happens when we get rich? Research has shown that even during the first year after a big win on the lottery, the winner's perception of happiness is the same as that of people who have not won. And investigations of people who have seen their income increase significantly have similarly shown that this does not lead to a higher degree of contentment.

The purchasing power of the average American more than doubled over a period of forty-five years. Did this lead to an increase in happiness? In 1957, 35 per cent of Americans said that they were 'very happy'. The corresponding figure in 2002 was lower, 30 per cent. Similar research in other industrialised countries has shown the same tendency: levels of contentment have not increased in the past fifty years, in spite of strong economic growth. Even if research has shown that certain indigenous peoples exhibit levels of contentment as high as the Americans, for instance, it is the norm that people's levels of contentment decrease below a certain economic standard. What is interesting, however, is that the levels of contentment in a population do not seem to increase once you get above a level of about £10,000 per year.

There have also been studies of academics being assessed for promotion within their universities. When they were asked how they would feel if they did not get the post they wanted, they often replied that it would mean that their lives would feel empty and pointless. When they were checked up on several years later, those who had failed to be promoted were roughly as happy as those who had been promoted.

So what goals are worth striving for if we want to achieve greater happiness and contentment? One study has looked at people's goals in life in relation to how happy they thought they were. It showed that the people who had struggled to get a high income and a successful and prestigious job were roughly twice as likely to describe themselves as relatively or very unhappy, compared to those who named close friends and a happy marriage as their most important goals in life. Similarly, research in forty-one countries demonstrated a close correlation between the perception of happiness and how highly people valued love. The more important people regarded love to be, the happier they were. For those who valued wealth most, however, the situation was the reverse. The more important money was to them, the more unhappy they were.

It is clear that we often chase goals that do not give us a sense of success when they have been achieved. It is important to differentiate between genuine and false goals for success so that we do not waste our time chasing mirages. And according to a number of studies it is clearly the case that material success seldom makes us happy, while good relationships give us feelings of satisfaction and success.

External and internal success

Where I live there is an athletics competition for children every year. Hundreds of parents take the opportunity to admire their children's various sporting talents and to cheer them on. Once I was standing by the finishing line of the 60-metre sprint, watching a boy whose parents I was slightly acquainted with cross the line in second place. The boy's father went up to him, and I was expecting him to congratulate his son, but instead I heard the following exchange: 'It's a shame you didn't win, but you can try again next year.' The boy carried on smiling, albeit slightly more stiffly, and replied: 'But I came second. That's pretty good!' Then the smile vanished when his father said: 'The only reason for taking part is to win.'

External success is about how we are perceived by those around us. We are evaluated according to the yardstick of another individual, our family or our society at large, and defined according to various criteria of success. Internal success is how we perceive ourselves. Here it is our own yardstick that counts, and our achievements are judged in relation to the demands we make of ourselves. And this is where our heart has its say.

The boy had lived up to his own interpretation of success by coming second, but this internal definition collided in a brutal fashion with the demands of what the world around him regarded as success, in this case represented by the boy's father.

It is not uncommon that internal and external perceptions of success are not the same. In the case of the boy and his father, the outside world had a narrower view of the term 'success' than the person responsible for the achievement. But there are also examples of the opposite.

The vast majority of people would agree that the Nobel Prize is one of the greatest indications of success a person can achieve. The French author Jean-Paul Sartre was awarded the prize for literature in 1964, but turned it down. For Sartre, the Nobel Prize was not a sign of success.

When we analyse our own success, we have a tendency to compare ourselves with others. It is not the case that we regard ourselves as economically successful just because we own more than people did one hundred years ago, or because we are richer than people in low-income countries. What counts are our successes in relation to those of our peers. In one study American students were asked if they would prefer to earn a certain amount of money each year while other people only earned half as much, or if they would prefer to earn twice as much money, while other people earned even more, twice as much as them. The result was that most of them chose the first alternative: earning less, but more than others. Our internal sense of success is therefore closely linked to comparisons with other people.

But these comparisons need not concern how things are going for other people. We also make comparisons with ourselves as the yardstick. Would we be happier with a silver medal than a bronze medal? The answer may appear obvious, because a second place is a better result than coming third. But research has shown that the opposite is in fact the case. Sportsmen who have won an Olympic bronze medal are often more content than silver medallists, who are more likely to fret over the fact that they did not win. In the same way, the team that wins the bronze medal in football's World Cup often leaves the tournament with a sense of success. They may have lost the semi-final, but they bounced back and finished the tournament with a victory. The silver medallists, on the other hand, have lost the final, and lost out on the title. We make comparisons with what might have been, and relate our situation to this.

This reminds me of a story about a man who lived with his wife and nine children in a little house with only one room. He went to a wise man and asked for advice because their situation was unbearable as a result of the overcrowding. 'The advice I give you is to bring the goat in and let it live with you,' said the wise man. The unhappy man wondered if he had misheard, but the wise man confirmed that they should bring the goat into the house, and asked him to come back after a week. When the man returned, he was asked how things were. He replied: 'It's hell. The goat stinks, it butts people, and takes up loads of space. It's terrible!'

'Good,' said the wise man. 'Now you can let the goat out again. It will feel as though you are living in paradise.'

Many aspects of our lives are probably like this. It is through comparisons that we judge how well we are doing. This is why an outdoor temperature of 15 degrees feels cold in September but warm in April.

How we perceive our own success can also be a question of self-confidence. If we have a strong belief in ourselves, we can never be positively surprised when we achieve successes which those around us think are impressive. If we have little faith in ourselves, we can think an achievement impressive while those around us think it commonplace.

Our self-confidence has its basis in several factors. Our

genes play a certain part, but our upbringing is also of decisive importance. Sigmund Freud said: 'A man who has been the indisputable favourite of his mother keeps for life the feeling of a conqueror, that confidence of success that often induces real success.' If we believe that we are invincible, it can improve our chances of succeeding with what we undertake.

Living with an internal sense of success, whether or not this is connected to the perception of the world around us regarding success, can be very positive. But this sense can also slip into something entirely different. There are people who are not successful in the eyes of those around them, but who believe that they are regarded by others as extremely successful, and who also feel an internal sense of success. When this discrepancy between reality and their internal perception of themselves becomes noticeable, this is described as a grandiose self-image, or megalomania. This inflated condition can be dangerous, both for the individual and for those around them, and is not uncommon in criminals.

A lack of self-confidence can also be a double-edged weapon. It may mean that all success comes as a pleas-ant surprise. But our lack of self-confidence can also fool us into thinking that nothing that we achieve is worth anything.

A lack of self-confidence can also affect us in another way. The desire to achieve more, to achieve new things all the time, never being completely content, can drive us onward, in the hope of showing that we really are good

enough. A blessing? A curse? How we handle this characteristic is up to each of us.

It is a question of finding a good balance. We cannot
simply rush through life without enjoying and appreciating
what we have. We are the ones who decide whether the
glass is half full or half empty. In the end it depends on us
deciding whether we want to be dissatisfied or satisfied with
what we've got. In December 1914, Thomas Edison's lab-
oratory burned down, and with it a lot of the prototypes
that Edison and his colleagues had been working on. The
loss of the building alone was not even covered by insurance. After looking at the devastation, Edison said: 'All our
mistakes are burned up. Thank God we can start anew.'

What is success?

So what does the word 'success' mean? Even if we can
agree on certain criteria for success, we will be forced to
conclude that each and every one of us must find his or
her own definition of the word. We have different views
of what is important in life, of the meaning of our existence, and we define the word according to our
relationship with this individual philosophy. My own view
of success would be: 'Success is a subjective experience
which can only be defined in our own hearts.'

To a large extent, ever since I was a toddler, my goals for
success have been laid out for me. I would become an

oncologist and cancer specialist. I would become a senior physician and a professor. And then I would become departmental head at the Karolinska Institute in Stockholm. And, with these career goals in mind, I strived for years. I became a specialist in the care of cancer patients, I became an associate professor at the Karolinska Institute, and ended up leading a large research group. Everything was heading in the right direction – until I went into a life-crisis in the mid-1990s. My views on what was really important in life were changed by this crisis.

When, as a result of these experiences, I decided that I wanted to write a book about God, I realised that this would be the end of my career as a researcher. My hopes of becoming a professor and departmental head would not be fulfilled, because writing the book would demand so much of my time (and I also thought that I would be regarded as some sort of 'nutter' by the research community because I had written a book about God). I had a lot of clever colleagues in my research group, and I would have to hand over a large part of the responsibility, and the honour, to them if I was to be able to write the book. After thinking about this for about a minute, I decided that this was how it would have to be. There were more important things than having a career, becoming a professor and departmental head, I thought. I had no choice – I had to write the book.

Once the book, *A Concealed God*, was published three years later, I looked around to see what had happened during those years. What I saw was surprising. It turned out that the research had never gone as well as it had done during those three years. My colleagues had proved themselves to be better researchers than me, and with support, advice and encouragement they had achieved great things. And the following year I was appointed full professor and departmental head, to my great surprise.

I had achieved all my goals for success, and the most remarkable thing is that as soon as these goals were no longer the most important thing to me, they were fulfilled. Perhaps it is like when you look at an object in the dark. If you look straight at it, you see it less well than if you were to look slightly to the side of it.

My years as head of the institution were very rewarding, but I could never get away from the feeling that it was more a question of a period of training, than something that would be my life. Maybe this was an external success, but was it an internal one? A couple of years ago I decided to resign as head of the institution, and straight after that I cut my hours as a professor to part-time and decided to leave the research I was engaged in and definitively hand over the group to my closest colleague, a very talented researcher.

I did this so that I could work on other issues instead, questions of ethics and about how we should live our lives. The following year *The Seventh Day* was published, a fictional story about the meaning of life. And I started to lecture on relationships and ethics on a regular basis.

This transition has not been (and is still not) easy. I

abandoned a secure career that would have provided for me until I retired, for a considerably less secure path, in both economic and career terms. But it still feels right. I know that what I was doing before was not quite right for me, and that what I am doing now feels meaningful. And, when it comes down to it, perhaps the feeling of living a meaningful life is one of the most important criteria of success.

KIND AND SUCCESSFUL

If we take the decision to succeed in life and to be successful – what should we do then? It is my belief that taking care of those around us – being kind to our fellow human beings – is a precondition for us becoming truly successful. True success is not achieved by those who are smart or inconsiderate, by hard-baked egotists or psychopathic bosses. Success in life is achieved in other ways. In most instances what we do purely for ourselves does not benefit anyone, while what we do for each other benefits everyone.

So what should we do to be successful? There are several concrete pieces of advice that we can follow. But it is interesting that in the end they can be reduced to two tips, which are actually entirely obvious, but also strangely undervalued – we should be kind, and we should use our kindness with discernment.

This advice applies to our working life, our social life and our inner life. All of these pieces need to fall into place if we are to be successful in our lives.

Generosity

A lot of people think of money and open-handedness when they hear the word 'generous'. Clearly, a willingness to share your money with others is a form of generosity. But it is not just a matter of distributing your money. Interestingly, though, there does seem to be a link between generosity in an economic sense and a general desire to share what you have. Mean people, on the other hand, tend to keep what they have from others in many different areas of life.

What does it mean to be generous? What characterises a generous deed, and differentiates it from other deeds – good and bad alike? Being generous means undertaking an act without asking for anything in return. There is no demand for an exchange, either of goods, services or money. Generosity is a one-way act without any expectation of getting anything back. What is remarkable is that generosity without any expectation of getting anything in return often pays off.

One form of generosity concerns sharing glory. When I decided to hand over part of the responsibility for research to my colleagues, I realised that at the same time I would have to let them take a large part of the glory.

They would receive recognition for having made medical discoveries, not me. Interestingly, as soon as I decided that this was how it would have to be, I felt a great sense of liberation. I no longer needed to look out for my own interests. I could allow myself to do things purely because they felt important. And because they were good for other people.

My father, Jerzy Einhorn, sometimes used to quote the American president Harry S. Truman's words: 'It is amazing what you can accomplish if you do not care who gets the credit.' And my father always worked according to this principle – do as well as you can, and be generous towards your colleagues. And so he became successful, as a doctor, as a researcher, and later as an MP and author.

We tend to guard our own preserve. We want to get credit for anything we do that is good. We, and no one else, should get the glory for what we have achieved. If we get too little appreciation, we get upset and feel as though we have been badly treated. And occasionally we even persuade ourselves that we should receive more credit than we really deserve.

This is a form of meanness. We do not want to share and be generous with glory in favour of others. But there is really no reason for concern. The world is so ingeniously constructed that everything evens out in the end. Sometimes we get less glory than we deserve, and sometimes we get more than we should get. So we can sit back and relax. What we lose on the swings we make up on the roundabouts. If we are generous with glory, we will gain, one way or another. The remarkable thing about glory is that however much we give away, it always comes back to us.

But we can also be generous in other ways, for instance with praise and encouragement. If you ask people whether they think they have been given too much praise and encouragement, hardly anyone would say that they have. But there are a lot of people who think they have not received enough encouragement.

It is interesting that so many people are starved of praise, when it does not actually cost anything to praise and encourage others. It is not as if we ourselves lose anything by giving someone else praise. It is something we can give away without it costing a penny.

There is a common misconception that there is a hierarchy which determines how praise should be distributed. So we expect that parents, teachers and bosses should give praise (even if they do not always do so), but not that children, students or colleagues should. This is wrong, of course, because praise and encouragement can move in any direction: upwards in the hierarchy, or sideways, or downwards. Children need encouragement from their friends, parents and teachers, but at the same time parents and teachers also need to hear that they are doing a good job. At work, we need to hear that we are doing well, from our workmates, our bosses, and from our subordinates.

I have noticed that a lack of criticism is occasionally

the greatest compliment one can receive in the work-place. When this is the case, it makes you want to cry. Praise is, after all, something which is entirely free, in all respects. It is a commodity which there is no good reason to ration.

But there is not merely a lack of encouragement and praise. We also need constructive criticism and feedback in order to grow and develop. And sometimes we are too sparing with good criticism.

What is good criticism? Three things characterise good criticism. The first is that it is given in private. The second is that it is given in order that the recipient should grow. If factors such as aggression, a desire to assert oneself or a lack of control over one's impulses form any part of it, then we should refrain from giving criticism – always! The third is that good criticism should be given with love. If you think this is too strong a word, you can swap it for 'sympathy' or 'consideration'. Out of thoughtfulness for our fellow human beings, we say what the other person needs to know in order to grow.

Should we tell someone that they have bad breath? Most people are quick to say that we should not. Sometimes we persuade ourselves that it would be inconsiderate to tell someone about this. Sometimes we admit the real reason to ourselves – that we do not dare, or, even worse, that we do not care. Someone who has bad breath and is not aware of it has an unconscious handicap which can some-times lead to social isolation. Telling someone about this problem can lead to a new start in life. Is cowardice a good enough reason not to give another person this chance?

Denying another person the chance to grow and develop is a form of meanness. We ourselves need good criticism, so we should be generous with it towards others. And when someone, out of love and concern for our development, gives us criticism and feedback, we should accept it with gratitude, however difficult it is to hear that we are not perfect. Then it is up to us how we choose to handle the criticism. We need not agree with everything, but what I have learnt from getting good criticism is that it often includes truths from which we can learn.

I have already mentioned that when we ask someone for advice, a situation arises in which both parties win. It is therefore a good idea to be generous with our requests for advice from other people. My experience is that if there is a potential conflict on the horizon, it can often be defused by asking the other person how we should best handle the situation.

Several years ago I contributed to developing a medical information package. When the work was almost complete, the clients started to question how the programme could be disseminated, and hesitated over whether they actually wanted the product we had worked so hard to develop. We called a meeting with representatives of the clients and asked them for advice about how to distribute the programme. The originally frosty climate became creative instead, and after the meeting we not only had a mass of ideas about how the programme could be used, there were also several among the clients who enthusiastically started working for the completion of the project.

A lot of people are worried about the impression they make on those around them. There is absolutely nothing wrong with this, as long as it does not become exaggerated. No one is perfect, and we all know that deep down. Another form of generosity is therefore to be open with our faults, mistakes and shortcomings. This is generous, because it helps other people to feel better about themselves.

There is a special characteristic which a lot of people have in secret. It is called the 'impostor syndrome'. It means that we believe we are surrounded by competent and clever people. There is just one exception – me. I am in reality not as clever and capable as the world around me seems to think. And the strange thing is that the world around me has not yet noticed that I am really just a good actor and an impostor. My big fear is that I will one day be discovered.

A lot of people suffer from the impostor syndrome. The best thing we can do to make people realise they are no worse than others is to be open about our own faults and shortcomings. And the best thing we can do for ourselves is to realise that people around us are not as superior as we sometimes imagine.

It is important to stress that this generosity with our faults and shortcomings must be used with discernment.

Few people appreciate masochists or self-deprecating behaviour.

We learn by imitating others. Since we were babies, this has been the way we have developed and learned new things. We did not learn to walk, use our hands and speak through secret correspondence courses – we learned by imitating other people.

The Japanese music teacher Shinichi Suzuki studied how the famous Japanese songbirds learned their fantastic song. It turned out that the breeders introduced into each room of newly hatched chicks a so-called master-singer, a bird that sang particularly beautifully. The small birds then tried to imitate the master-singer, with mixed results to start with. But gradually their song became more beautiful, until eventually they invented their own themes. Suzuki used this technique when he developed a method based upon imitation which has since helped millions of children to learn to play various musical instruments.

Human beings' original way of learning is through imitation, and this is how we continue to learn throughout our lives (obviously complemented with often boring school studies and even more boring homework). As adults we have not lost the ability to learn through imitation. Studies have shown that people talking to one another repeatedly imitate each other's postures. People have also had electrodes attached to their faces and then been shown photographs of people with different expressions. The muscle groups activated in the faces of the participants were the same as those activated in the faces of the people in the photographs when they were smiling, or looking angry, for instance.

It is unfortunately the case that our attitude to learning by imitation changes as we grow older. As adults, we are expected to gain knowledge without imitating others. Imitation is even regarded as something shameful. 'Stop copying' is a phrase we will all have heard, along with the insult 'copycat'.

This is an expression of a remarkable way of thinking. We have good chances of developing our generosity by allowing others to learn from what we are good at. And if we are generous in teaching what we can do, we should not be afraid to learn from others by imitation. And if we are generous towards others in this respect, it is considerably easier to get generosity in return.

But how do we act towards people with whom we have not yet had the chance to share our generosity, but from whom we would like to learn something? Well, we should say exactly how it is. 'I think you're so good at . . . Can't you show me how you do that?' Most people will then be happy to share their knowledge.

Do not be ashamed about imitating others. Ask how other people do things. Try to think your way into how they think. Learn from others, and be generous with teaching others. Imitating is allowed. Curiosity is allowed – it is even a good thing.

★

One form of generosity is particularly difficult to develop: being generous in feeling joy at other people's successes. It can be the case that we compare ourselves with others and hope that they fail, so that we can feel that we are not so bad. This may concern work, studies or sport – sometimes we just do not want other people to be more successful than us.

We can learn to think in different ways on this issue. And we ought to think in different ways, because there is nothing to be gained by not being generous with feeling joy at other people's successes. On the contrary, those around us can often sense that we are being envious, no matter how much we try to hide it by commiserating with them on their failures (often with poorly concealed schaden-freude) and stiffly congratulating them on their successes. Do not forget that those around us often have more sensitive emotional antennae than we think.

Besides, if we are happy about other people's successes, then we will have a lot more to feel happy about than if we only feel happy at our own successes.

Why should we be generous? Why not, like the Western careerists we often are, just take what we need and ignore what happens to everyone else? Can we not simply – to use a rather extreme phrase – trample over bodies in order to further our own success?

As well as all the ethical reasons for acting fairly towards our fellow human beings, there is one reason which, perhaps more than any other, should motivate us to be generous – we ourselves gain by being generous towards those around us.

How is it possible that generosity towards our fellows can lead to us succeeding better in life? One reason is that a generous person is not regarded as a threat by those around him or her. When people do not perceive any competition, they themselves stop competing and instead start to cooperate, which everyone benefits from.

Another reason is that if we are generous towards those around us, they will be generous in return. As has already been mentioned, there are studies which show that we are inclined to be generous towards those who are themselves generous. Even if their generosity is directed towards someone else, it gives rise to a desire in us to be generous towards them. What you give comes back to you, one way or another. The author Mark Ortman said: 'One of the most difficult things to give away is kindness, for it is usually returned.' And it is not only kindness that is difficult to give away – the same applies to all forms of generosity.

A third reason to be generous towards other people is that we get pleasure from it. Our brains are programmed to give us satisfaction from doing good for others. And a lot of people would agree that it is more fun to give away a present that is appreciated than it is to receive a fine present yourself.

A fourth reason is harder to summarise. It is as if there was a natural law which ensures that generosity and good-will get their reward. And perhaps this is not so strange. In

Mark's Gospel it says: 'whoever wants to become great among you must be your servant, and whoever wants to be first must be slave of all.' [10:43–44] Naturally we should not be each other's slaves, nor diminish ourselves entirely, but these words still contain a truth, that if we work from the intention of making life a little better for others, then we ourselves will also grow as individuals. If we learn to take pleasure from others' successes, this attitude is sufficient for us to get recognition for what we ourselves have achieved. One way or another, we get our reward. This is kindness in one of its best forms – serving others. And at the same time we are also serving ourselves.

Generosity is a great way of showing your kindness. I have described several ways in which we can be generous – there are many more. Generosity benefits others and it benefits us ourselves – always a winning combination. So be generous, not least for your own sake. And remember – in the end, it is not *why* we do good for our fellow human beings that counts, but that we do it.

Seeing others

In the 1930s the Austrian physician René Spitz visited a children's home where there were many children but few staff, which meant that the children hardly ever got any attention. They were kept clean and fed, but had very little human contact. Almost all the children appeared apathetic and underdeveloped, and some had already withered away and died, without anyone understanding what disease they were suffering from. Strangely, there was one child who seemed well and who was growing and developing.

Spitz investigated why this was the case. It turned out that a cleaning lady used to clean the dormitory while the children were asleep. When she had finished cleaning, she always sat down on the bed closest to the door, picking up and cuddling the child who lay in it. Just for a short while – every night. In that bed lay the only child who had developed normally. Spitz has written several interesting research papers on children in children's homes. He has shown that children who do not have emotional contact develop more slowly and more often die prematurely than children who receive attention from the world around them, but it is rather unclear if this particular story is entirely true. But, in any case, it illustrates a truth – that we can do a great deal for our fellow human beings merely by seeing them.

Children must be seen and loved in order to grow up and become mature and responsible individuals. Food and clean clothing are not enough. Without love the little child shrivels up, both physically and emotionally. If we are not seen enough as children, we risk becoming emotional invalids as adults.

Not only children need to be seen in order to develop and grow. The same applies to adults. If we are not seen, we shrivel inside. And if we are not heard, we do not develop our innate potential. The father of psychoanalysis, Sigmund Freud, said: 'Psychoanalysis is in essence a cure through love.' And this is surely the case – that we can heal our fellow human beings by seeing them.

Have you ever experienced any of the following situations?

- You are talking to someone at a dinner party, asking about his life and listening with interest as he talks about his thoughts and experiences. When you break up, he has not asked you anything and knows nothing about you.
- You are relating a story from your life to someone else. As soon as you break off to draw breath, she starts to tell a similar story (sometimes not even similar) from her own life.
- You are talking to someone who is looking away the whole while, and who is clearly thinking of something completely different.
- You meet someone you know in the corridor, and are just about to say hello when you notice that the other person is staring at the floor.

Most of us have experienced some or all of these situations, which are indications of a certain lacking in our society.

Every day consists of encounters. We encounter our fellows at home, at work, at school, on the bus, in restaurants, on walks, at parties, in shops and so on. And each time we decide what we want from this particular encounter. We choose if we want to relate to the person we encounter as an object or as a person.

Every day we talk to a lot of people. Sometimes the conversation lasts a few seconds, sometimes several hours. And each time we choose how we listen. We can choose not to listen, to listen with one ear or to listen with our entire being.

Seeing another person means being present with the whole of our being. And this is how we should aim to live our lives, in contact with our fellow human beings and the world around us. Every day – many encounters, all of them offering an opportunity. For the other person, and for us ourselves. It does not take any longer to be present in these encounters, to see and listen to another person, than it does to relate to them on a routine level.

A child can appeal to us to be seen and looked after in an obvious way. If this does not work by being cute, it will always work by screaming until the child gets attention. It is not so simple for adults. We cannot crave the attention of the world around us. The only demand we can make is of ourselves – to see and listen to other people.

Even as children we learn that 'curiosity killed the cat'. But why should it be a bad characteristic to be curious? It is naturally one of the preconditions for us seeing other people and understanding their inner lives. The problem with the society in which we live is not that there is too much curiosity. On the contrary, there is far too little.

Sometimes you hear the argument that someone is too tired. 'I'm too exhausted to listen' is a phrase we have surely all heard, and occasionally uttered ourselves. But of course this is not true. We do not lose energy by paying attention. We do not wear ourselves out by seeing another person. On the contrary, we gather energy from encounters to which we contribute in a meaningful way. Seeing a person is a form of kindness. And, as usual where genuine kindness is concerned, we benefit from it ourselves.

To conclude, an extract from a poem by Tomas Tranströmer, about the remarkable things that can happen in a genuine encounter:

> It happens but seldom
> that one of us really sees the other:
> for a moment a person shows himself
> as on a photograph but more clearly
> and in the background
> something which is bigger than his shadow

Conflicts

The word 'conflict' comes from the Latin word 'conflictus', which means 'collision'. It can be defined as 'a state of opposition which demands resolution'.

We can all end up in conflicts: at work, at school, in our families, with our friends, in rush-hour traffic. Sometimes it is said that conflicts are constructive. That quarrels and serious clashes are necessary and important – that they give us a chance to develop and grow.

I do not agree. Conflicts are, in my opinion, generally

destructive. Exchanges of opinion, heated discussions and debates can certainly be constructive. Different ideas and compromises often contribute to our development. But conflicts – when people get angry with each other – destroy more than they construct.

There are usually only losers in conflicts. The only thing we can learn from conflicts is how to avoid them in the future.

So how should we handle the potential conflicts that we all, sooner or later, end up in? One clue to how we might act in these situations was suggested by my youngest son when he was only three years old. He and his elder brother had been fighting for hours when my wife and I decided to teach our children a lesson. We decided that they would not be allowed to watch television that evening, but would have to go to bed early. When we told them, of course they started to protest loudly, but we were immovable. They were going to be taught a lesson, so both boys had to go to bed without watching any television. After a little while, our eldest son came into the living room and said: 'You're stupid!'

'Yes, yes, yes,' we replied. 'Go back to bed.'

Soon after, his younger brother came in and we were expecting the same sort of comment, when he opened his mouth and said: 'I love you.'

Our hearts melted at once, we interrupted our educational effort, and he rescued an evening of watching television not just for himself, but also for his brother.

What had my three-year-old son understood, but many

adults still not seen? That the best way of handling conflicts is usually with a measure of kindness, tolerance and – why not? – love.

We all have this opportunity. Next time we can all try to counter an aggressive attack with friendliness and objectivity, and watch how a potential conflict dissolves into nothing and we are left standing there as victors. Not in the conflict, because we will have avoided that, but as victors over ourselves.

Of course there are exceptions, but they are extremely rare. It is almost never worth the cost of having a conflict, so for our own sake and everyone else's, we should try to handle the next approaching conflict with insight. I am not suggesting that we flee any nascent conflicts, but that we should handle them with great wisdom.

We should be pragmatic in the face of a threatening conflict. We must ask ourselves: Where do I want to get to, and how can I get there? The obvious answer is almost always that we want to avoid gaining another enemy. We always lose by having enemies.

The conflict may be about who does more washing up and cleaning at home, about decisions that need to be taken at work, about how long our children should be allowed to stay out in the evening, or about the fact that a friend has let us down. The conflict can be resolved if we plan a strategy to reach a conclusion that everyone can live with, and a good solution almost never means that we part as enemies.

We should also try to shift our perspective and see the

whole problem from the other person's point of view. When I lecture on medical ethics, I sometimes do an exercise with the participants. An ethical dilemma is presented to them, and they each have to prepare the defence of a point of view, and then debate it with a participant defending the opposite opinion. Then they have to swap roles, and argue the other point of view. Often something remarkable happens – suddenly we understand the problem from a broader perspective.

We often lock ourselves into one point of view for fairly obscure reasons, and are incapable of shifting our perspective. Training in how to change our point of view not only increases our chances of solving conflicts, but also increases our own wisdom.

Yet another advantage of trying to put ourselves in the other person's situation and perspective is that we then increase our chances of actually *seeing* the other person. An almost endless number of conflicts have their basis in the fact that people feel they are not being seen.

We often approach a conflict with a desire that the other person will change either their attitudes or their way of behaving. This can be particularly apparent in relationships where people are living close together, such as in a family. But a lot of people have taken it upon themselves to change another person, only to fail completely.

The only thing that we really have any chance of changing is ourselves. And the remarkable thing is that if we work with ourselves as the tool, instead of trying to alter the other person, we might actually see a change in the other person, as a consequence of our own changed behaviour. People can change, not because someone tells them to, but because they themselves decide to change, sometimes after being inspired by those around them.

It is well known that the people with whom we have most difficulty are those who possess characteristics we ourselves have within us. This represents a fantastic opportunity, because we have a choice. Either we use our irritation or anger to express our aggression by attacking the other person. Or we use these feelings to understand ourselves better. What is the less likeable characteristic I share with this person? Can I do something about this characteristic, which I evidently do not appreciate?

Within Buddhism it is said that we should be grateful to our enemies, because they teach us tolerance and self-awareness. And this is true. Each time we approach a conflict, we are also approaching an opportunity: to understand ourselves better, and to train ourselves in the difficult art of treating our fellow human beings in the best possible way. Seeing the conflict as a challenge that we can use to train ourselves is undeniably better than being gripped by the discomfort and the primitive feelings many of us experience before a fight.

There is no research that shows that we get rid of our aggression by screaming and arguing, or letting our anger out in other ways. It is not the case that aggression is collected and released through a safety valve if only we are allowed to scream and be a bit mean towards those around us. On the contrary, several studies have shown that outbursts of aggression can lead to an increase in our anger.

One option is to reduce our agitated feelings by physical exertion. We can run a few kilometres, do an aerobics session or hit a punchbag. The relief that many of us feel afterwards can be interpreted as us having vented our aggression. A more probable explanation is that it is the tiredness that comes after physical exertion – and the simultaneous release of endorphins (which make us feel good) – which is doing the work.

Another option is to use this energy in another direction. We can channel our anger into something constructive by taking this force and using it for something useful. We can actually decide ourselves how we want to use this energy. Perhaps we could channel it into sympathy for the person with whom we are in conflict. Or for greater self-awareness. Or for planning how to solve the problem that the conflict illustrates. This is not easy, but it does work, if we decide to go down this path. And it is a fantastic sensation to free yourself from negative feelings, which are only a dead weight in life.

So should we always be kind in conflicts? Are there no situations when it is right to fight? Of course there are situations like that. If we see someone being attacked on the street, it might not be suitable to speak to the attacker in a friendly way. If a genocide is under way, our politicians ought not merely to consider various economic sanctions. There are situations, even if they are rare, when we must use force. But there is always an afterwards, when we must do what we can to create good relations. One example of how badly things can turn out – and how well – is the aftermath of the two world wars.

After the First World War, a peace treaty was signed in Versailles which left a disarmed Germany with a great loss of land, a large economic debt to the rest of the world and a deeply damaged self-image. This humiliation eventually gave rise to Nazism and the Second World War, with the immense loss of life entailed by that.

After the Second World War, the USA made a great effort to rebuild Germany and the rest of western Europe. The Marshall Plan helped to create an economic and social infra-structure which made it possible for the defeated country to begin to reconstruct its self-image and resume its place among the nations of the world. And this help to European countries in turn led to an improvement in the American economy.

Once again, this is a question of kindness linked to a good deal of judgement which benefited all parties. We can avoid or deal with most conflicts, and this is some-thing which benefits all of us. Negative feelings towards our fellow human beings are primarily damaging to our-selves. And if we try to harm others, the usual result is that we are also harmed.

Bitterness, wounded pride and anger are not things that we enjoy feeling. But the fantastic thing is that we have the opportunity to liberate ourselves from these negative experiences of the world. And the first step is the most important – to decide that we no longer want to feel like that.

We all carry with us a cargo of old injustices. It may be a question of things we have done to other people. And it may be a question of those that we ourselves have been subjected to. Sometimes these events took place many years ago, but the bitterness nevertheless remains.

There is a Buddhist story about two monks who had to wade across a river. A young woman was standing at the ford, worried about how she would reach the other side. One of the monks offered to carry her across on his shoulders. The other monk thought that it was outrageous that he should come into contact with a woman's body like that, but said nothing. Once they had reached the other side, and the woman had thanked the monk for his help, they continued their journey in silence. Eventually, as evening approached, the other monk could no longer hold back, and reproached his colleague for carrying the woman across the river. The monk who had carried the woman looked at him in surprise and said: 'Are you still carrying her? I put her down several hours ago.'

Bitterness and aggression become a burden that we drag with us through life if we do not come to terms with these feelings. The most irreconcilable hostility can be transformed into its reverse by a process of reconciliation. Many years of bitterness between members of the same family can be transformed into closeness and fellowship. Many years of war have been followed by close cooperation

and understanding. But all of this requires a process of forgiveness and reconciliation.

In 1990 Nelson Mandela was released after twenty-
seven years in prison. The South African apartheid regime
had reached the end of the road, and democratic elections
were announced. After his years in prison, Mandela showed
himself to be a free man in more than one sense. He was
not bitter and vengeful, but was instead concentrating on
the future. He went on to be elected president, and was
awarded the Nobel Peace Prize in 1993. Mandela was
willing to forgive and be reconciled with his old oppon-
ents, and has as a result become an example to anyone
who has been subjected to injustice and persecution.

It can sometimes be difficult to apologise. It can be difficult to forgive. Reconciling ourselves with what has
happened can require a lot of internal work. But in the end
we will be the biggest winners if we can take that step, even
if many years have passed. There is a lot of energy locked
up in these old conflicts. If we decide to come to terms
with them, this energy is released, and can be used for
other, more important things. If we apologise and forgive,
we become more liberated people. If we are reconciled with
what has happened to us, we grow as individuals.

Empathy

One research project has looked at how people want to
be treated in the event of severe cancer. One of the ques-

tions asked was whether they would be willing to undergo intensive chemotherapy with serious side effects if there was a chance of being cured, and how small the chance of a cure might be for people still to agree to the treatment. When healthy people were asked, the average response was that they would refuse treatment if the chance of being cured was less than 50 per cent. When the same question was posed to people who were about to begin treatment for cancer, they replied that a 1 per cent chance of a cure would be enough to make them want the treatment.

This research shows that when we are healthy, we believe that we would not want treatment for cancer if the chance of being cured was not good. But when we develop cancer, we think entirely differently. We will often take any opportunity of becoming healthy, because hope is usually the last thing that leaves us.

We think differently at different times of our lives, and sometimes we cannot even imagine how we would react in a different situation. We can ask people how they would act if they stood in front of a burning building, and discovered that there was a small child inside. Would they risk their own lives and rush in to try to save the child? The answer is that we do not know how we would act until we find ourselves in front of the burning building.

In our daily life we relate constantly to other people. And we all want to be treated according to our own needs. But if we do not even know how we would act at another stage of our lives, how can we put ourselves into someone else's thoughts and emotions? Saying 'I know just how it feels' to another person is a form of intolerance, because it assumes that we all share the same inner world, which of course we do not. But our task is to understand as well as we can.

As we have seen previously, there are also great cultural differences in how people think. Fons Troompenaars has looked at how people think they would act in the following imaginary scenario: 'You are riding in a car driven by a close friend. He hits a pedestrian. You know he was going at least 35 miles per hour in an area of the city where the maximum allowed speed is 20 miles per hour. There are no witnesses. His lawyer says that if you testify under oath that he was only driving 20 miles per hour it may save him from serious consequences.'

In the USA and most west European countries, a large majority of respondents said that they would not lie under oath to save their friend. In Sweden only 8 per cent said they could imagine giving false witness. In France, however, the corresponding figure was 27 per cent, and in Russia and Venezuela, for instance, more than half said that they would lie to protect their friend. Similar differences in how we think have been revealed by other studies.

So there are differences in how the same person thinks at different stages of their life, in how different people within the same society react and behave, and in how people from different cultures think. This is not a question of who is right and who is wrong. It is just that people's ways of reasoning vary between different societies. This fact underlines how important it is not to assume that everyone is the same as us. Instead, we should try to put ourselves inside the other person's world.

How can we do that? There are only two possibilities for us to understand another person's thoughts, feelings and needs. One is to ask them how they feel and how they want to be treated. The other is to try to imagine how that person thinks and feels. This capacity for understanding – empathy – is available to all of us, to a greater or lesser degree. Everyone gains by having a good ability to imagine the emotional world of our fellow human beings. It creates the preconditions for treating our fellows as well as possible – at work, within our families, among our friends.

In the research described previously, general practitioners and nurses were also asked how they would feel about being treated for cancer. The most common response from nurses was that they would refuse treatment if the chance of being cured was not at least 50 per cent, whereas the corresponding figure for doctors was 25 per cent.

It goes without saying that if health professionals were to treat patients in the way that they themselves would want to be treated, then it would turn out wrong, time after time. Instead, they have to be able to put themselves in their patients' place, and understand their needs and their internal world.

We all want to be treated with consideration and respect, so it is important that we treat those around us in the same way. And empathy is an ability that we can develop throughout our lives, if we only decide to. How can we train ourselves to become more empathetic? There are various ways of developing the ability. Here are a few possibilities.

The first and greatest step towards becoming a more empathetic person is to decide that this is what we want. Once the decision has been taken, we can devote days on end to developing this ability. Every encounter with another person is a training opportunity, and, as a rule, every day consists of many encounters.

The next possibility is to try to put ourselves in another person's shoes, and imagine their world, asking ourselves questions like: What are they thinking? How do they want me to act? What is important to them? And when we have tried to answer these questions, we should ask the person in front of us what they are thinking. In this way we can get feedback, and, as usual when we are learning something, we need feedback in order to develop. And do not worry too much that the person you meet might think you intrusive. The vast majority of people enjoy talking about themselves.

Buddhism has meditation techniques which are specifically intended to foster greater compassion and empathy towards those around us. With these techniques you train yourself, for instance, to think good of other people, and to identify with them. Meditation is an undervalued resource in the Western world. Not only can it give us greater empathy, but it can also give us inner peace, greater energy and increased insight.

The method described earlier, where we swap roles in a discussion and argue for the directly opposing point of view, is another technique we can use to develop our empathetic ability. If we consciously try to imagine how another person is thinking, we are simultaneously training our empathetic ability.

In the same way, our empathetic ability benefits from listening to and seeing those around us. The more we learn to exploit every opportunity to see our fellow human beings, the more we develop the ability.

In the end, it is a question of self-awareness. Even if there are differences between people, we often think in similar ways. If we learn to recognise our own internal world, we will simultaneously learn more about other people's needs, wishes and problems. But, at the same time, it is important to remember that we are not all the same.

Developing our empathetic ability is no small task. It is a constant challenge, and we will never reach the end of our training, but it is a challenge that is worth accepting.

Responsibility

We bear responsibility for a lot in our lives – merely saying that we have to take responsibility does not tell us very much. What I mean here is the bit of extra responsibility beyond the usual. It is about exceeding expectations; it is about 'over-delivery'.

Several years ago my family was on holiday in a hotel in

Italy. It was a well-run hotel, but one incident in particular filled us with delight. The children had taken with them an entire suitcase full of cuddly toys, which we had to drag with us throughout the trip. Upon returning to our rooms after a day at the beach we discovered that the cleaners had been in. And they had done something beyond the usual call of duty. They had positioned the stuffed animals in a circle on the bed, so that it looked like they were having a meeting. The children were delighted, as were we adults.

When we got back to the hotel the next day, the children rushed into the room. They were not disappointed. The cleaners had once again thoroughly cleaned the room, and had then lined up the animals on the floor so that it looked like they were forming a train. One of the animals was missing. It was in the bathroom with a toothbrush in its paw.

What had the cleaners done? They had certainly done their job satisfactorily. And then they had given a few per cent extra. It had taken little extra time and effort, but it had made our family very happy (the initiative led not only to a lot of happiness, but also to a large tip – and remember, it is entirely acceptable to do good deeds for selfish reasons). This is precisely what over-delivery is.

After working as a director for several decades, one of the things I have learned is that colleagues can be divided into three groups. When the members of the first group are given a task, they do not do it entirely satisfactorily. This is a small group. There is a large group which does the task in an entirely adequate way, often very well. And then there is a small group which, when given a task, does it well, and then goes on to give a few per cent extra. This group has hit upon a path to success.

So should we work an extra five hours each week in order to be successful? No, we should *not* take everything upon ourselves, and we have the right to say no sometimes. But what we do undertake to do, we should do really well. Whether it concerns work, family or friends, we should take responsibility for what we have undertaken, and then do a bit more.

Every person's deeds count, and spread out like ripples on a pond. In this way our deeds have consequences not only for our immediate vicinity, but for an endless number of other people. And in this way our responsibility for the world around us is extremely large. And we are the ones who decide if we want to live up to this responsibility.

Being a role model

Since we were children we have learned from role models. We have examples whom we imitate. If we learn that it is all right for other people to scream when they get angry, we will also scream when we get angry. If we learn that it is good not to be generous, we will also learn not to be generous. If we see that it is acceptable not to show understanding, then there is a great risk that we ourselves will live our lives without showing understanding. And if we see those around us treat us and others with understanding, kindness and compassion, we will learn to treat others in the same good way. We each have role models whom we attempt to imitate – parents, siblings, friends, teachers and so on.

We should not imagine that this changes when we grow up. We still have role models whom we attempt to imitate, consciously or unconsciously. This role model may be a boss we look up to, a partner, a celebrity or a close friend. It is important that we choose our role models with care. But it is just as important that we ourselves can be role models for others. We are the examples who others try to imitate and copy. This may concern our children, our colleagues, our friends. Around us we have people who look up to us and would like to be like us.

It is a great responsibility that we bear throughout life – being an example to others. Because it is not always the case that people act in a certain way because we tell them how to act. It is much more common for them to act in a certain way because they have seen other people acting in that way.

The fact that we act as examples can also have negative consequences. Medical students' abilities to develop empathetic attitudes towards their patients have been studied. The results showed that their empathetic ability could actually decrease during the course of their training, in certain courses. This probably arose from certain of their teachers, their role models, having a non-empathetic attitude.

Good examples – in family life, at school, at work – can do immense good for those around. In this way, kind and good behaviour extends outwards. This applies not least to managers, who can see directly how exemplary behaviour spreads throughout their organisation.

The author Malcolm Gladwell discusses in his book *The Tipping Point* how changes take place in human society. He draws the conclusion that changes in behaviour often happen because certain key individuals start to act in a particular way at a certain point, and that this changed behaviour spreads through society as a form of epidemic.

An example is the dramatic decrease in the crime rate in New York during the 1990s. The number of murders, for instance, decreased by two-thirds, and the number of violent assaults by half. This may in part be the result of a reduction in the drug trade – primarily in crack cocaine – and a decrease in the rates of unemployment, but this is not enough to explain the dramatic change. Instead, it is thought to have been the result of certain people in important positions adopting a particular strategy to deal with the situation. Instead of focusing on serious crime, they chose to deal with problems like vandalism, litter, graffiti and fare-dodging on the subway.

This sent a signal out to society that there was zero tolerance of *all* crime. And when key individuals within the criminal fraternity realised that crime no longer paid, this thought in turn spread like an epidemic. This meant that everyone began to follow laws and rules to an increasing degree.

In this way the behaviour of individual people under specific circumstances can lead to a dramatic change of behaviour in many more people. The wonderful thing about this thought is that one person really can change the world.

The world consists of pen-givers and pen-takers. The pen-givers are those whose pens have always disappeared, and they are always looking for a new one. The pen-takers are those who have ten pens in their pockets and desks full of pens which people have for some unknown reason 'forgotten' there.

But the world also consists of energy-givers and energy-takers. Energy-takers steal our power, but without themselves getting stronger. Energy-givers share their power with us, but without getting weaker. We choose our own path – and we can choose to be a powerhouse and an example to others, an energy-giver.

We look at others and others look at us. We imitate others and others imitate us. We influence many people's lives and many people influence us. It is a big responsibility to be a (fellow) human being.

It can't be that easy to change? – about self-awareness and development

A person is not one-dimensional and static. We are not unchangeable and rigid. A person is like a crystal. We exhibit different facets of our personality depending on which side is being illuminated. Each person has a thousand strings to his or her bow, and we decide how we want to play at any given moment. This means that we can say 'I am always myself' and mean it, at the same time as we exhibit highly varying behaviour depending on the circumstances we encounter.

This in turn means that we need not alter our personalities. It is more a matter of choosing which aspects of our personalities we would like to shine most strongly. We cannot change other people, but we can change ourselves, and in this respect we have unlimited power.

It is important to recognise a few simple things which we have a general tendency to forget.

- We are always part of the problems we experience.
- We have great power to contribute to their solution.
- We can learn a lot on the way, and grow as individuals as a result.

If we want things to be different in our lives, then we ourselves have to take responsibility for that. No one else can do it for us. And if we see hindrances ahead of us, we must decide if they are real or merely excuses for the fact that we lack courage.

How do we start this process? The first step is to make the decision to change. And not only to make that decision in our minds, but also in our hearts. The next step is to stop and take the time to ask ourselves a few questions.

We have to be self-reflexive. Examples of these questions might be these.

- Am I doing right by myself?
- Am I treating others right?
- Am I doing the right things?
- Why am I doing them?
- What do I think is important and meaningful?

It is important to take time now and again (not all the time) to think about where we are, who we are and where we are going. In the temple at Delphi there was an inscription in gold letters above the door: *Gnothi seauton* – 'Know thyself'. Self-awareness is a precondition for inner development, whether it be a matter of worldly or non-worldly goals.

One method for examining if we have found the right path in life is to do one of two mental exercises. The first is: 'If I were seventy-five years old and looked back on my life, would I be content?' If the answer is yes, then we are on the path to success. If the answer is no, then it is time to think again.

The second mental exercise is: 'What would I do if I only had one year left to live?' If we decide that we would continue more or less as we have been doing, then we are on the right track. Otherwise we may have to think things through once more.

In this reflection it is not always the case that we will get clear answers, but this is not the most important thing.

The most important thing is the process itself. In this way, the path is also the goal.

Self-reflection is an important element of the path towards success. We have to stop and ask ourselves whether we are heading for a goal which is important in our hearts. Far too often we feel that things are not as they should be, but for various reasons we dare not change course from one that feels secure, or sometimes just familiar.

The psychiatrist Viktor Frankl stressed that success does not come because we strive for it, but because we strive to do what feels meaningful to us: 'I want you to listen to what your conscience commands you to do and go on to carry it out to the best of your knowledge. Then you will live to see that in the long run – in the long run, I say! – success will follow you precisely because you had forgotten to think about it.'

I believe Frankl is right. Far too many people strive for career goals, only to find when they achieve them that they feel empty. And then they set off after new goals, only to experience the same feeling once they get there. If we instead concentrate on what feels meaningful in our hearts, this feeling will not arise, but rather a feeling of direction and meaning. We cannot hold on to anything if our hands are clenched.

When we strive for things that feel important to us, we can sometimes experience a feeling of being 'carried'. We can feel that within us there are forces about whose existence we had no idea. People sometimes talk about never believing themselves capable of carrying out a task or dealing with a difficult situation, but that when it was most needed, the power to do it was there. Discussing where this strength comes from is not the purpose of this book, and I do not have any sure answers anyway. Let us just conclude that people are capable of a very great deal when they need to be, and when the purpose is good. And that it is worth striving for that particular feeling of meaning and direction.

It is important to stress that what is meaningful for one person need not be what a lot of people would consider great and impressive. It may instead be a question of feeling that the work we do with other people is important. Or that we feel the significance of caring for our children. Or helping a friend in need. Or planting a tree.

Helen Keller, who became blind and deaf at an early age but who nevertheless learned to communicate with the world around her, and later became an advocate for human rights and peace, once said: 'I long to accomplish a great and noble task, but it is my chief duty to accomplish humble tasks as though they were great and noble.' We can all find meaning in 'humble' things.

I do not mean that we should all build a great city or plant a forest or write an opera that will be premiered at the Met in New York. I do not mean that we should all become international superstars recognised and idolised by millions. Or Nobel Prize winners. Or Olympic gold-medallists. Nor is it the case that people who achieve fame always perceive their lives as meaningful.

Life is endlessly rich and meaningful. The problem is that we are often in so much of a hurry that we do not have time to appreciate the significance of everything we encounter and all that we do. We do not always see how much of what we do is meaningful and important. For this reason we need to stop and look about us in order to recognise it. We need to strive for that particular sense of meaning.

Sometimes seriously ill patients speak of how meaningful they think life is, when they do not have long left. They can see the meaning in a beautiful day, in birdsong, or in an everyday encounter with another person. And this is indeed the case – a lot of what we take for granted contains great meaning and beauty. It is just that we do not always have time to see, listen and reflect.

So how can we find what is meaningful for us? We have to look for the answer within ourselves, and we must set aside time and energy with which to look. We must give ourselves time for reflection. Sometimes we have a lot to gain by asking the advice of those around us and by getting a chance for reflection in the presence of other people. Another person's perspective can make the difference when we feel that we alone are not capable of finding a solution.

When I was seventeen I started to smoke. My parents, who were both cancer specialists, were naturally unhappy about this, but I did not care, because I was determined to smoke! When I had been smoking for about three years, I felt a small lump at the back of my mouth. After a few weeks I went to my father and asked him to have a look and tell me what it was. He looked in my mouth, then looked me in the eye and said in a serious voice: 'Stefan, you have a precancerous lesion.'

I stopped smoking immediately, and since then have never had any problems with lumps in my mouth. And to this day I wonder what my father actually saw in my mouth. But he got me to stop smoking. Sometimes the ends justify the means.

What my father also succeeded in doing was to use an external influence to create an internal motivation within me. In the end it is internal motivation that drives us forward to do a particularly good job or to take an important decision. Other people cannot directly motivate us to do this, but they can influence us so that the special generator of internal motivation gets activated.

But we do not always need to reflect together with others. Sometimes we just need to give ourselves time to be alone. In the collective society in which we live today, we seldom get time to ourselves – time to reflect, encounter ourselves properly and ask ourselves questions about who we are, where we are going and why. It is no easy task to take on, but, as Tomas Tranströmer wrote: 'In the middle of the forest is a glade which can only be found by someone who is lost.'

Sometimes, not very often, perhaps, you get to read small pearls of wisdom on toilet walls. The following wise words, which I read and quickly wrote down, come from the wall of a public toilet, and underline a fact that is well worth thinking about: 'I have never met anyone who on their deathbed wished that they had spent more time at the office.'

CONCLUDING REMARKS

Why should we be kind? Why should we be good? Why should we be ethical? The answer is that there are many reasons for us to do good. Here are some of them.

- We feel better if we do good. Research has shown that it is pleasurable to do good things for others.
- The people around us feel better if we do good things for them. Being surrounded by people who feel good is enjoyable, and helps us to develop.
- Indirectly we create benefits for ourselves by doing good things for others, because what we do for others comes back to us, one way or another.
- Societies with widespread ethical thinking function better than others.
- We will get a better world as a result. Even if individual people can sometimes feel powerless, this is not the

case. Do not forget how the effects of a good deed can spread out like ripples on a pond. We can do more than we think for others, and in this way make our contribution to a better world. And a good world is much better to live in than a bad one.

In the end we have everything to gain by being kind with discernment, and a lot to lose by not being kind. And this is no bad reason for being kind – the fact that we ourselves gain by it. In fact, this is a really *good* reason.

The American film *It's a Wonderful Life* by Frank Capra is one of my favourites. In the film we meet a man, played by James Stewart, who lives in a small town. He wants to leave his hometown and travel around the world, get an education and embark on grand projects. But his departure is constantly postponed, and instead he has to work in the small family firm, giving mortgages to the weaker members of society.

Many years later his world collapses when he is unable to repay a loan in time. Just as he is about to commit suicide, so that his family can have his life insurance, an angel steps into the story and shows him all the bad things that would have happened to the people in the town if he had not been born. The end of the film can bring tears even to the eyes of really tough guys (which includes me?) when we see how the people he has helped over the years now join forces to save him.

The film does not just show that we have everything to

gain by doing good for others, but also how we can affect other people's lives by our actions. Our responsibility for other people is vast. It can feel overpowering to think about it. But this fact ought rather to fill us with a sense of meaning and responsibility. And in the end it is true that all we can do is our best.

The American president Theodore Roosevelt once said: 'The most important single ingredient in the formula of success is knowing how to get along with people.' I agree – nothing we can do to promote a successful life is more important than having the ability to relate to our fellow human beings in a good way. We become complete individuals in our encounters with others, and it is in our relations to those around us that we are measured and judged. By others – yes, this is true, but this is not the most important aspect. The central issue in the end is who we are to ourselves, and to everything that humanity means.

Another American president, John F. Kennedy, said in his inauguration speech in 1961: 'Ask not what your country can do for you. Ask what you can do for your country.' We can apply these wise words directly to ourselves and to our relationship with those around us. 'Ask not what your fellows can do for you. Ask what you can do for them.' With this attitude we will get back much more than if we make demands of those around us. With this attitude we will achieve success in our lives. Because it is quite simply the case that we become successful by making others successful.

There is a story about the wind and the sun arguing about which of them was strongest. They decided to find out by competing to see who could make a man walking along a road take off his coat. The wind blew as hard as it could, but this only led to the man clutching on to his coat even more tightly. Then the sun shone brightly. The man got hot and took off his coat.

This is probably reflected in reality: if we want to achieve something, we will have considerably greater chances of succeeding if we are warm and affectionate than if we are aggressive and violent. As the Swedish children's character Bamse, the strongest bear in the world, once put it: 'Better being kind than strong.'

In South Africa there is a particular phrase, *ubuntu*, which is difficult to translate into a Western language but concerns the very core of being a human being. The Nobel Prize winner Desmond Tutu, in his book *No Future Without Forgiveness*, wrote this about ubuntu: 'A person with ubuntu is welcoming, hospitable, warm and generous, willing to share. Such people are open and available to others, willing to be vulnerable, affirming of others, do not feel threatened that others are able and good, for they have a proper self-assurance that comes from knowing that they belong in a greater whole.'

I wonder if I have ever seen a better description of the word 'kind'.

The English author and philosopher Aldous Huxley said towards the end of his life: 'It is a bit embarrassing to have been concerned with the human problem all one's life and find at the end that one has no more to offer by way of advice than "Try to be a little kinder".' In the end it probably really is this simple – and this difficult: kindness is the greatest thing we can offer those around us, and ourselves.

SUGGESTIONS FOR FURTHER READING

For anyone who wants to continue to explore the noble art of being kind, there are a great many books from which to take inspiration. Here are some suggestions of books which deal with questions of how we can live a good life.

Buber, Martin: *I and Thou*. Continuum 2004.

Frankl, Viktor E.: *Man's Search for Meaning*. Rider & Co. 2004.

Gladwell, Malcolm: *The Tipping Point*. Little, Brown 2000.

Kushner, Harold: *When Bad Things Happen to Good People*. Pan 2002.

Mandela, Nelson: *Long Walk to Freedom*. Abacus 1995.

Nørretranders, Tor: *The Generous Man*. Thunder's Mouth Press 2005.

Rinpoche, Sogyal: *The Tibetan Book of Living and Dying*. Rider & Co. 2002.

de Waal, Frans: *Good Natured*. Harvard University Press 1996.

Young, Jeffrey E. & Klosko, Janet S.: *Reinventing Your Life*. Plume 1994.